# Introduction to
# Japanese
# Culture

edited by Daniel Sosnoski

## Tuttle Publishing

Boston • Rutland, Vermont • Tokyo

All photographs on the cover and in the text of this book were taken by Narumi Yasuda, except for the photographs on p. 27, p. 30, p. 48, p. 54, and p. 57, which were taken by Hidé Doki, and the photographs on p. 28, p. 40, which were taken by Frank Leather.

Published by Tuttle Publishing,
an imprint of Periplus Editions (HK) Ltd.,
with editorial office at 153 Milk Street, Boston, MA 02109

LCC Card No. 96-62169
ISBN 0-8048-2056-2

First edition, 1996
Fourth printing, 2001


Distributed by:

*Japan & Korea*
**Tuttle Publishing**
RK Building 2nd Floor
2-13-10 Shimo-Meguro, Meguro-ku
Tokyo 153 0064
Tel: (03) 5437 0171
Fax: (03) 5437 0755

*North America*
**Tuttle Publishing**
Distribution Center
Airport Industrial Park
364 Innovation Drive
North Clarendon, VT 05759-9436
Tel: (802) 773 8930
Fax: (802) 773 6993

*Asia Pacific*
**Berkeley Books Pte. Ltd.**
130 Joo Seng Road
#06-01/03
Olivine Building
Singapore 368357
Tel: (65) 280 1330
Fax: (65) 280 6290


Printed in Singapore

# CONTENTS

## List of Line Illustrations

# PART ONE

# Holidays
# and Festivals

# *SHOGATSU*

## New Year's Day

IN JAPAN, as in other Asian countries, the New Year's holidays have always had a special significance. They are by far the most important—and the longest—holidays in the Japanese calendar. For almost a week the bustling Japanese economy practically comes to a standstill. Schools, companies, and stores close down; and trains, planes, and highways are packed as millions make their way to their hometowns or to ski resorts and *onsen* for the festivities. From December 30, when the holiday actually begins for most people, huge cities like Tokyo, Osaka, and Nagoya take on an eerie quietness until the great rush back home and a return to the office starts on January 4 or 5.

The holiday is especially a time for family and friends. It is also a time for parties, reunions,

formal visits, and a host of New Year's celebrations and games that give the season its special flavor. Just like holidays in other parts of the world, one of the special activities is lots of hearty eating and drinking along with good fellowship and cheer. Traditional New Year's foods are prepared well in advance to minimize cooking and household chores. For example, *mochi*, a thick, gooey cake of pounded, cooked rice, is prepared so that it can be served at breakfast, lunch, or any other time of the day. And *osechi ryori*, a seemingly endless array of cold tidbits served from stacked lacquerware boxes, is prominently featured at all New Year's meals—from simple snacks to elegant banquets.

Traditionally, New Year's preparations have included ritual housecleaning, the clearing up of all debts, new kimono for each child in the family, and the hanging of special decorations. These ancient customs are still carefully preserved by many Japanese families. A walk down any quiet street during the holidays reveals a fascinating blend of the old and the new: *kadomatsu* decorations, made of bamboo stalks and pine boughs, standing beside the shuttered entrances of skyscrapers; Shinto *shimekazari*, straw ropes strung with little angular strips of white paper, hanging across the front of parking lots, supermarkets, and electronic game centers. Even though the symbolism of some of these customs may be lost to many people, to Japanese the holidays would never seem the same without them.

In these and many other ways, New Year's in Japan is really quite similar to the holiday season in Western countries. Where Americans send Christmas greetings to their friends, Japanese exchange New Year's cards. Because of the special extra crews hired by the post office just for this purpose, Japanese receive their greeting cards all at once on New Year's Day itself if the postman is on time. And the custom that many Americans observe by attending church on Christmas Eve finds its counterpart in Japan, where a visit to a Shinto shrine or a Buddhist temple is traditional during the early hours of New Year's Day. Many people, especially women and children, dress in *kimono* for these *hatsumode* visits, a beautiful custom that makes the season even more festive.

# SETSUBUN

## Bean-Throwing Ceremony

THERE ARE probably many foreigners in Japan who first learned of *setsubun* after the startling experience of seeing Japanese friends or acquaintances throwing beans around for apparently no reason. Most Japanese can probably offer at least a superficial explanation for this custom, but there are also doubtlessly many who have never given serious thought to the full significance of *setsubun*. Observance of this holiday may actually be declining.

As a traditional custom, *setsubun* is preserved in part by somewhat nontraditional means. TV and movie personalities, for example, publicize the event by appearing in front of well-known shrines to throw beans. Other bean throwers to which the media may turn are sumo wrestlers, otherwise known for their salt throwing. Celebrities thus serve to remind the Japanese of their cultural heritage, even if the busy public takes little or no time to reflect on it. Many holidays are rooted in the celebration of the seasons and are easily lost in the shuffle of modern urban life. For most Japanese office workers, holidays are significant only if they provide a day off; their original meaning or purpose is in most cases either forgotten or irrelevant.

Still, holidays are preserved and remembered not by their meaning but rather by the activities associated with them. Though few Japanese are likely to know or think about the origin of *setsubun*, there are many who faithfully follow the custom of scattering beans on February 3. Originally, when the lunar calendar was in use, *setsubun* took place at the beginning of spring, as the name suggests. To shout "*Oni wa soto, fuku wa uchi*" was therefore not only a kind of prayer, but also an affirmation of a new beginning: out with old troubles, in with new hope. The Japanese make much of New Year's cleaning, but even in February there is probably much of the same spirit among those who follow the *setsubun* custom

today, regardless of whether they really believe that they are driving away demons.

*Setsubun* is related to *tsuina*, originally a Chinese custom introduced in Japan around the beginning of the eighth century. Some participants in the ritual, which took place at the end of the lunar year, wore masks representing various demons that the others were to drive away by screaming loudly and shooting arrows into the air. The tossing or scattering of beans (*mame maki*) appears to be a fairly recent practice, dating from the Muromachi period.

A similar ritual in the West is observed at weddings in the tossing of grain at newlyweds to encourage fertility. At Christian weddings, for instance, grains of rice are thrown. The symbolism of beans, grain, and rice originates in the life and values of a predominantly agrarian society. Custom preserves the symbols but not necessarily their meaning.

Concern with demons and particularly the wearing of masks can be compared with the Irish and American custom of Halloween, even though this holiday, October 31, marks the end of summer rather than the end of winter. Primary school children, disguised as ghosts, witches, and monsters, go from door to door asking for treats. Halloween ("All Hallows' Eve") is the night before All Saints' Day. The original celebration of Halloween goes back before the coming of Christianity, but according to later tradition it signified the last night on which the powers of evil could freely roam the world before the Christmas season. To this extent, the spirit of Halloween is rather similar to that of *setsubun: oni wa soto, fuku wa uchi.*

# HINA MATSURI

## Doll Festival

MANY JAPANESE as well as foreigners might be surprised to learn that the story of the *Hina* Festival, Japan's major festival for girls, is a relatively recent one. The name of this festival probably comes from *hiina,* a Heian period game that used dolls, doll houses, and models to mimic court life. Although the game had no direct relation to the present-day *hina matsuri,* the word *hina* came to be used for describing paper dolls and later became associated with the Doll Festival, supposedly in the Edo period. The festival seems to have become firmly established by about the mid-seventeenth century. Two or three paper dolls were placed in the *tokonoma* together with rice cakes and other special foods. During the Edo period the doll collections became more and more elaborate, evolving into displays that had three, five, and finally seven steps and that were more than a meter high. Standing dolls gave way to sitting dolls mounted on wooden bases, and paper dolls were replaced by elaborately clothed dolls with ceramic heads and hands. During the Meiji era the number of dolls continued to increase, although many of the new characters had little relation to the original *Hina* Festival.

In the 1920s department stores began selling the dolls in complete sets. Today the prices of these sets range from $500 to $5,000 and more. Prices are determined by the size of the dolls, the quality of the clothing, whether the dolls are ceramic or plastic, and by the fame of the dollmaker. The sets are handed down from mother to daughter or are presented to a newly born girl by the mother's parents. After World War II sets of two dolls in glass cases became popular, perhaps due to space limitations.

On a display of seven steps that have been draped with a piece of red cloth, one might see the following collection: On the top step there may be a doll house resembling a palace, but more often there is a folding golden screen decorated with paintings of pine, plum, or bamboo. In front of this sit dolls representing the emperor, dressed in dark clothes, and the empress, in a red, twelve-layer kimono. On the second step are three court ladies. Below these there is a five-member band composed of a singer, three drum-players, and a flute player. On the fourth step may be two guards as well as rice cakes in colored layers of pink, white, and green; and on the fifth, attendants carrying slippers and umbrellas. On the sixth step may be various pieces of furniture. Finally, at the bottom, may be a model of a carriage or a palanquin and miniature models of flowering cherry or orange trees. The scene calls to mind a banquet or wedding celebration, and the furniture and carriage suggest the dowry of a girl marrying into a noble family. While each individual piece is quite beautiful, the total effect may appear rather cluttered. But it is a reflection of the manner in which the individual pieces have been added to the display over a period of time.

Doll displays are set up about a week before the March 3 festival, and children take great pleasure in assembling the dolls, putting on headpieces or placing instruments in the dolls' hands. When the child is still too young to do it, the mother sets up the doll collection, and she may have her hands full keeping the children from disturbing the display and damaging the dolls. The dolls are there to be admired but not to be played with; they are not toys. Following the festival, the dolls are promptly put away, since leaving them out too long is said to result in delaying the girl's future marriage.

# Common Dolls and Figures

1 **hina-ningyo:** doll set

2 **dairi-bina:** royal couple dolls

3 **sannin-kanjo:** ladies-in-waiting

4 **gonin-bayashi:** court band

5 **nagashi-bina:** paper dolls

6 **gogatsu-ningyo:** Boy's Day dolls

7 **nobori:** banner

8 **kabuto-ningyo:** samurai doll

9 **Shoki:** Chinese mythical hero doll

10 **Momotaro:** fairy tale hero doll

11 **Kintaro:** boy warrior doll

12 **fuji-musume:** wisteria-girl doll

13 **yamato-ningyo:** doll of powdered wood

14 **gosho-ningyo:** court doll

15 **kimekomi-ningyo:** wooden doll with cloth kimono

16 **Takasago:** Noh play dolls

17 **uba:** old woman in Noh plays

18 **jo:** old man in Noh plays

19 **kokeshi:** wooden doll

20 **maneki-neko:** lucky beckoning cat

21 **hariko-no-tora:** papier-mâché tiger

22 **daruma:** papier-mâché Bodhidharma

23 **shishi-gashira:** lion-dance head

# HANAMI

## Cherry Blossom Viewing

THROUGHOUT the world, the transition from winter to spring is celebrated annually in rituals ranging from Easter parades in the West to cherry-blossom viewing in parts of the East. For almost 2,000 years now the traditional Japanese rite has been to celebrate the brief appearance of their favorite flower, the *sakura*.

Along with the plum, pine, and bamboo, the cherry blossom has been completely assimilated into the life of the Japanese people, from art to literature to *hanami*. *Hanami* is the name given to the cherry-blossom-viewing parties that begin in southern Kyushu and continue northward through the archipelago as warm weather ushers in spring. The pale, perfectly formed cherry blossoms last only a week or so. For the Japanese they are synonymous with the transitory nature of life itself and the brief duration of youthful beauty.

Like the rose in the European Middle Ages, the *sakura* was claimed initially by Japan's privileged classes. Early Japanese emperors led courtiers, warriors, and royalty in selecting viewing sites where poets and artists entertained the assembled guests with artistic celebrations of the cherry blossoms' fragile beauty. The tradi-

tional *hanami* of the upper classes appear to have reached their zenith in 1598, when Hideyoshi the Regent gave his famous *Daigo no Hanami* near Kyoto. Hideyoshi had invited all the powerful *daimyo* of the land to what was to be his last blossom-viewing party. That same year he died, and with him an era disappeared. With the coming of the Tokugawa Shogunate under Ieyasu, many of the customs followed by Japan's privileged classes were democratized.

*Hanami* were no exception to this general trend. Generally, the more refined viewing of earlier times was replaced by an emphasis on eating, drinking, dancing, singing, and general merrymaking. In popular literature from poetry to *kabuki* plays, the *sakura* and *hanami* were frequent themes. Artists, too, were inspired by blossom-viewing. In *ukiyo-e*, for example, it is clear that *hanami* had become an integral part of the life and manners of the common people.

While no two blossom-viewing parties are alike, most include the same activities that were begun during the Genroku era. Once they have located a suitable tree, jubilant groups of people sit down under the blossoms and begin their feast. Hours later, drowsy from singing, dancing, and consuming saké and *bento* (lunches), they return home on trains and hired buses.

In Japan, as in other countries, the spring flower-viewing has always included an important symbolic note: the annual rebirth of nature's growing season. For Christian countries, at least, the key spring ritual, Easter, has religious roots. For the Christian it is the Easter lily that expresses the joy of spring. Other traditions associated with spring are not as filled with historical and cultural meaning. Many people head for nature trails and wilderness areas to view spring tree buds and wildflowers. Some wear new, bright-colored clothing in annual parades. And still more put away the winter sports equipment to make room for spring's recreational pursuits.

These days baseball, tennis, golf, and track and field have almost surpassed Easter and *hanami* in popularity. Nonetheless, few Japanese would miss April's blossom-viewing. For no other event can take them back so completely to their historical, cultural, social, and psychological roots.

# TANGO-NO-SEKKU

## Boys' Day

MAY 5 IS Boys' Day. *Tango-no-sekku*, as it is called, is celebrated to motivate young boys to become spirited and healthy. On this day, cloth carp banners are seen flying throughout Japan because the carp symbolizes the epitome of indomitable will. Parents hope that their young sons, seeing the banners flying in the wind, will be inspired by the carp's fighting spirit. Carp are known for their tenacity, steadfastness, and willingness to surmount nature's obstacles. They are such spirited fish that they have been seen swimming up waterfalls and against swift currents.

The giant cloth carp seen flying over roofs or on poles are not only bright in color, they are very long. Some approach nine meters in length, and they are hung with even longer red and white streamers. Huge cloth carp banners are more prevalent in open, rural areas where they can fly freely in the wind.

Inside the house on Boys' Day, the *tokonoma* usually becomes a center of visual delight for young boys and their guests. The selected area becomes a showcase for masculine dolls that represent famous heroes from Japanese history and legend. Usually included in the exhibit are miniature helmets or *kabuto*, miniature suits of armor or *yoroi*, swords, bow and arrows, and other martial items, some of which are beautifully embellished with gold and lacquer. Also included in the display is *chimaki*, a sweet rice cake shaped like a cone and wrapped in a bamboo leaf. On Boys' Day the *chimaki* is served and eaten. Another special food for this day is a rice cake that contains *anko*, sweet bean paste, and is wrapped in an oak leaf. This confection is called *kashiwa mochi*.

The custom of *tango-no-sekku* originated in China in the seventh or eighth century, then spread to Korea and Japan. It was celebrated in all three of these countries, but in Japan there was a martial influence on the festival. Samurai families during the Edo period placed battle flags and streamers along with other trappings of war in front of their homes on this day. The martial decorations became an important element in the displays that were set up inside the home.

Also closely associated with Boys' Day is the Japanese iris, or *shobu*. Thus May 5 is sometimes called the Festival of the Iris. On this day people take hot baths in water containing iris leaves. This ancient custom was born of the belief that iris leaves have the power to drive out evil spirits. Some public bathhouses open early on May 5 and place fresh green iris leaves in the hot water. The aroma of the fresh leaves makes the water very inviting. In ancient times, iris leaves were also thought to have the power to put out fires. The custom of placing iris leaves on the eaves of houses as talismans against fires is still occasionally observed in some rural areas on May 5.

These are some of the decorations and symbols to be seen on the 5th of May. What is more impressive to the foreigner is that the day has, since ancient times, been set aside for boys. It can be seen as a sign that the Japanese respect the nature of children and are deeply committed to promoting their happiness and proper development.

# BON

## Buddhist All Souls' Festival

THE JAPANESE custom of *bon* probably has its origin in the *Avalamba Sutra* (*Urabon kyo*), which tells the story of Mokuren, a disciple of Buddha. Mokuren wished to help his deceased mother, who had fallen into the hell of hungry spirits (*gakido*). Buddha instructed him that if one practiced almsgiving and honored the three treasures of Buddhism (Buddha, the sutras and the priesthood), one could relieve the suffering of one's ancestors in hell for the preceding seven generations. With this instruction came the establishment of a time for honoring the dead in the middle of August (July on the old lunar calendar).

*Bon* is the time of the year when, according to Buddhist belief, the spirits of the dead return home to visit. Other religions also teach that after death one's spirit continues to live on, but the soul is not thought to return to this world. Tales of spirits visiting the living exist in the West in the realm of superstition and ghost stories, and generally have little religious foundation or support. The Roman Catholic Church does, however, teach that the living can, through prayer and sacrifice, aid those souls waiting to enter heaven. The Church celebrates two festivals in honor of the dead. In the first, All Saints' Day, children used to honor those in heaven by clothing themselves as saints. But now, on the eve of that day, children dress up as ghosts and goblins for what has become Halloween. Two days later the Church cele brates All Souls' Day in memory of all the dead, including those souls that are waiting in purgatory. Masses are said, and in some countries Catholics go to graveyards and place lighted candles on relatives' graves.

At *bon*, Japanese Buddhist families clean their houses and on August 13 go to the family graves. There they pour water over the gravestones, light incense and lanterns and leave flowers. Then they return directly home, escorting their ancestors' spirits to the family altar (*butsudan*). There a special meal of small dishes is set out, cultivating the feeling that the spirits are actually present. After three days, ceremonies are performed for sending the spirits to heaven once again. Fires are sometimes lighted in front of houses, and lanterns are set afloat in rivers to wind their way downstream and show spirits the way back.

For this very special festival, millions of Japanese return to their home towns. Tokyo seems quiet and nearly abandoned. The highlight of *bon* in all cities and towns is the *bon odori*, or dance. People gather for three nights and dance in a circle around a wooden platform that is decorated with lanterns. To the accompaniment of traditional drum and flute music, singers perform folk songs that may sound very strange to foreign ears, with the lyrics of the songs often being improvised. Although the dance repeats the same steps again and again, with dancers waving their arms and clapping their hands, the beautiful spectacle of it all keeps it from becoming boring. Men and boys wear *yukata* (cotton kimono) of white and navy blue, while women and girls wear *yukata* of all colors. Adding to the festival atmosphere are booths that sell goldfish, toys and masks, fireworks, candy, snacks, and drinks. The foreign visitor may want to try a Japanese soft drink called *ramune*, served in a bottle with a glass marble in its neck. Viewing the dance, the bright *yukata*, and the lanterns, the foreigner is likely to feel that this is one of the few times that the real Japan is on display.

# AKI MATSURI

## Autumn Festivals

IN FEW PLACES in the world does one nation spend so much time in joyous worship! Like adventurers flying west into an eternal sunset, the Japanese honor deities, nature, their relatives, culture, and history almost 365 days a year. Among the oldest *matsuri*, or festivals, are those belonging to the fall, or *aki*. Shintoism, the original pantheistic religion of Japan, inspired the majority of the country's *aki matsuri*, although several significant Buddhist traditions are also honored in September, October, and November. Often, traditional ceremonies combine the religious spirit of Shinto folk faith with rituals derived from seasonal planting and harvesting of Japan's rice crops.

The exact origins of each locale's festival are often only dimly recalled. But the unfolding of events has changed little over generations. The *matsuri* usually takes place under the sponsorship of a local shrine. Once or twice a year, in the spring and fall, the *ujigami*, or local spirit, is said to visit the fields from its home in the mountains. Thus *yama-no-kami* descends to become *ta-no-kami* and takes up residence in the shrine. On the festival day, the spirit is housed in a portable shrine called a *mikoshi*. Usually these are ornately designed miniature shrines attached to long wooden poles.

The men parade the *ujigami* through local streets in a turmoil of sound, lantern light, pageantry, artistry, and hedonistic fervor. Children, men, and women in traditional dress swell the ranks and add their dancing, singing and playing of musical instuments to the celebrations. *Matsuri* are distinguished from one another by spectacular additions such as the burning of giant bonfires during Kurama's *hi matsuri*, the October 22 Fire Festival. At Nagasaki's Suwa Shrine, the *okunchi* fills three days with many dances of Chinese origin, including the dragon dance. At Himeji's *kenka matsuri*, *mikoshi* "quarrel" with each other for supremacy. And finally, giant *dashi* floats called *yamagasa* in the form of lions and modern-day storybook characters fill the streets of Karatsu during the annual *okunchi*.

The details of the tens of thousands of *matsuri* would fill volumes. But among the most exceptional are those that break somewhat from the traditions of the Shinto observances. Kyoto, capital city of Japan for more than ten centuries, annually recalls its history in the *jidai matsuri*, or Procession of the Eras, that originated in 1895. Men and women in authentic dress portray the people of periods from the Heian period to the Meiji Restoration. All pass in front of the Heian Shrine and before thousands of viewers.

Tokyo is not without its festivals either. Two or three times during November, for example, citizens are reminded of the approaching New Year's holidays during the *tori-no-ichi*, or Fowl Market. Those anxious to guarantee good luck during the new year can purchase *kumade*, or good-luck bamboo rakes. Earlier in the fall season, Tokyoites can buy *chigibako*, a toy set of three boxes, or more important, fresh ginger at the Shiba Daijingu Ginger Festival. *Oeshiki*, the Commemoration of Nichiren, is another occasion for celebration in Tokyo.

Whenever a festival occurs, in fall, winter, spring, or summer, the feeling is always the same. Miraculously, modern commercialism has not touched Japan's *matsuri* in the same way it has blemished Western Christmas, Easter, and Valentine's Day. The most striking feature of a Japanese festival is its atmosphere of authenticity.

# SHICHI-GO-SAN

## The Seven-Five-Three Festival

PERHAPS the best words to describe Japan's *shichi-go-san* festival which takes place on November 15 each year are "charming" and "pretty." Westerners visiting Japan at this time invariably tell everyone of being enchanted by the spectacle of thousands of little children, with many of the girls dressed in brilliantly colored kimono and the boys in the somber, formal pleated skirts known as *hakama*, gaily clacking up the stone paths leading to Shinto shrines. *Shichi-go-san* (literally "seven-five-three") is a festival marking what Japanese see as critical ages in a child's development. Therefore parents take children who are seven, five, or three years old to shrines or temples to offer thanks and ask for future blessings.

Although the origin of the event is obscure, old records tell us that similar festivals have been celebrated in various parts of Japan for well over 400 years. Many of these celebrations

were not unlike various "rites of passage" that have been observed for children at certain ages in other cultures. Among the Japanese, young children were regarded as gifts of God until they reached the age of seven, at which time they became normal human beings. For a girl the age of three marked the first time that her hair would be put up in adult fashion; at the age of seven she would be given her first *obi*, the silk sash that is worn with kimono. And five-year-old boys would be given their first *hakama*, a traditional, formal kimono that some Japanese men still wear on special occasions.

The modern *shichi-go-san* festival was established during the Edo period. Interestingly enough, however, the holiday was largely confined to the Kanto area until fairly recent times, when department stores, confectioners, and children's clothing manufacturers started working aggressively to promote the idea as a nationwide festival. The occasion is very much akin to holidays such as Mother's Day, Valentine's Day, and other special days in America—not to mention Christmas—which seem to have a special meaning for merchants and greeting card makers. Although *shichi-go-san* is not a legal holiday in Japan, it still is an event that many people, especially children, look forward to with great anticipation.

Nowadays it is common to see many young children making their shrine visits in Western clothes rather than kimono. This is especially true of boys, as even the most doting parents find that miniaturized—and expensive—*hakama* have little practical value. But regardless of what they wear, most will be dressed in brand-new clothes and shoes or *zori* (sandal-like footwear) and will be given *chitose ame* candy or other sweets and good luck charms at the shrine. Many children will also receive gifts of toys, candy, and clothing from family and friends to mark this special day.

In some ways *shichi-go-san* resembles the way Easter is celebrated in the West. Although basically a religious holiday, Easter is also a time when children receive new clothes and baskets of candy from the "Easter Bunny." Clearly, parents of every nationality still find a wealth of opportunities to make holidays special events for children.

# PART TWO

# Arts and Skill

# CHANOYU

## Tea Ceremony

ALTHOUGH the foreigner may be unaware of it, the walk to and from the tea ceremony forms no less a part of the experience than the tea ceremony itself. The essence of the tea ceremony is harmony, and the tranquillity unfolds with each step the guests make toward the appointed place for this unique event. The garden path is first swept clean and then leaves or pine needles may be strewn along the path to the teahouse in order to add naturalness to the setting.

The classical tea ceremony had its origins in the thirteenth century when Zen Buddhist monks, in an effort to remain alert for their religious duties, passed the tea cup among themselves. However, it was the sixteenth-century devotee Sen no Rikyu (1522–91) who raised the ritual to a fine art. His influence on the ceremony was profound. Essentially a man of the Momoyama culture, Sen no Rikyu carried the tea ceremony to its austere limits. The ultimate setting for this master was a stark two-mat teahouse (*chashitsu*) that could accommodate only two or three people. Humility and

poverty were the standards passed down by Sen no Rikyu.

Chanoyu, the tea ceremony, is uniquely Japanese. Perhaps no encounter with Japanese culture leaves the foreigner more impressed, and less informed than the tea ceremony.

In the teahouse the guests kneel in silence on the tatami mats facing the *kama* (tea kettle) and the *furo* (brazier). The room is a hallmark of simplicity of taste. Perhaps a few flowers are arranged in an unassuming manner that adds to rather than accents the room. An appropriate scroll may be hanging in the room as a refined reminder to all present that their thoughts should be focused on what is about to occur.

The host then enters with the tea ceremony utensils and arranges them in an artistic and harmonious pattern. The motions of the performer are silent and remarkably economical. As the host proceeds to clean the implements the observer is aware that the scene itself and the *chashaku* (bamboo teaspoon), *natsume* (tea caddy), and tea bowl are immaculate. With these careful motions the cares and concerns of the outside world are left behind. It is at this stage that the Western visitor has either entered into the spirit of the ceremony or has found that the kneeling position is a rather uncomfortable distraction.

The sight of the finely ground tea is augmented by the swishing sound of the *chasen* (bamboo whisk) blending the water and the tea into a froth. All these ritual movements aid the participants in focusing their attention on the ordered movements of the ceremony. The same bowl is shared by all the participants, adding to the effect of a shared event. When the tea bowl is passed, the guest raises it and drinks all of the liquid. Here the foreign guest may not be aware that one is supposed to be attentive to the bowl as well as to the tea. A gentle compliment by the guest regarding the bowl is a normal part of the tea ceremony.

A simple ceremony may last only twenty minutes. The foreign visitor should try not to become lost in the formality of the ceremony and in so doing miss the simplicity of the tea ceremony's closing. Later, the host quietly departs from the room leaving the guests to reflect on their experience.

# A Teahouse and Tea Ceremony Setting

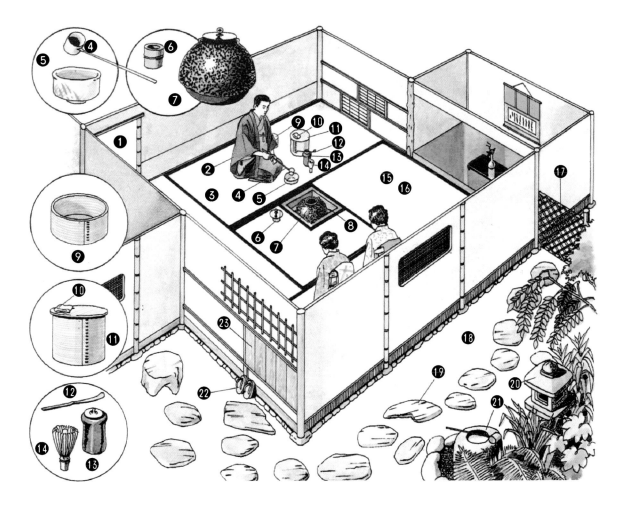

1  **sado-guchi:** tearoom entrance for host or hostess

2  **teishu:** tea-ceremony host or hostess

3  **dogu-datami:** place where tea is served

4  **hishaku:** bamboo ladle

5  **chawan:** tea bowl

6  **futa-oki:** kettle-lid rest

7  **chagama:** large iron kettle

8  **ro:** a low hearth

9  **kensui:** rinse-water container

10  **chakin:** tea cloth

11  **mizusashi:** fresh water container

12  **chashaku:** tea scoop

13  **chaire (natsume):** tea caddy

14  **chasen:** tea whisk

15  **chashitsu:** tea room

16  **yojohan:** four-and-a-half-mat room

17  **chumon:** small, bamboo gate

18  **roji:** pathway to tearoom

19  **tobi-ishi:** pathway stepping stones

20  **ishi-doro:** stone lantern

21  **tsukubai:** stone basin

22  **roji-zori:** bamboo sandals

23  **nijiri-guchi:** low entrance for guests

# IKEBANA

## Flower Arranging

THE WESTERNER who wishes to appreciate traditional Japanese art has few problems with the forms these arts take. Though one may not become a life-long fan, it is easy to appreciate the spectacle of Kabuki and the restraint and elegance of Noh. Both these forms have certain parallels in the Shakespearean and classical Greek theaters in the West. Traditional painting such as *sumi-e* and the screens (*byobu*) of an artist like Korin have equivalents in the stark modern Western abstract movement and the lush, decorative paintings of the impressionists. The art of *ikebana*, however, presents unique difficulties.

Of course, people all over the world take pleasure in growing and viewing plants and flowers. Sending a dozen roses as a gift to a friend or even cutting and combining various colored blossoms to match the decor of rooms or to add interest to a table setting is a common practice.

These Western standards are related to a cultural background that is quite different from Japan's. In Japan many of the arts continue to reflect the strong influence of Buddhism, a religion that stresses the impermanence of all

things and the beauty and pathos of change. Western art, with its strict distinction between art and nature, permanence and change, reveals a strong Christian influence in its emphasis on immortality and the desire to capture eternal beauty in the art object.

The origin of *ikebana* in Japan dates from about the seventh century, when the custom of offering flowers to the Buddha entered Japan from China and Korea along with the introduction of Buddhism. This was followed by a long period of development that culminated in the sixteenth century with the establishment of *ikebana* as an art in itself, independent of Buddhism. This development is usually credited to the Ikenobo school, which created the *rikka* and *shoka* styles. These incorporated religious and moral concepts as well as landscape symbolism in elaborate arrangements, some reaching a height of seven to ten meters, others stressing the beauty of a camellia or chrysanthemum.

The art of *ikebana* came to be organized in schools under the *iemoto* system. Since the creation does not last and, unlike a painting or sculpture, cannot be sold, it is the school rather than the individual that preserves traditional forms and develops new ones. Thus *ikebana* as an art is similar to music or to dance. The tradition or "score" is held in common; individual works are more like performances than objects.

Moreover, unlike Kabuki, Noh and other traditional arts that have settled on a fixed repertoire, *ikebana* has changed with the times. In the late nineteenth century the Ohara school developed the *moribana* style to reflect the growing use of Western plants and a more Westernized style of life. *Ikebana* came out of the *tokonoma* and became a more integral part of everyday life. In the twentieth century the Sogetsu school pioneered freestyle arrangements that incorporated abstract and surrealistic elements.

At a contemporary *ikebana* exhibition, works will range from the most formal classical ones to modern works that incorporate glass and metal on a monumental scale. This reflects the enormous variety of schools that provide instruction to over one million regular students both in Japan and in foreign countries.

# Setting for Flower Arranging

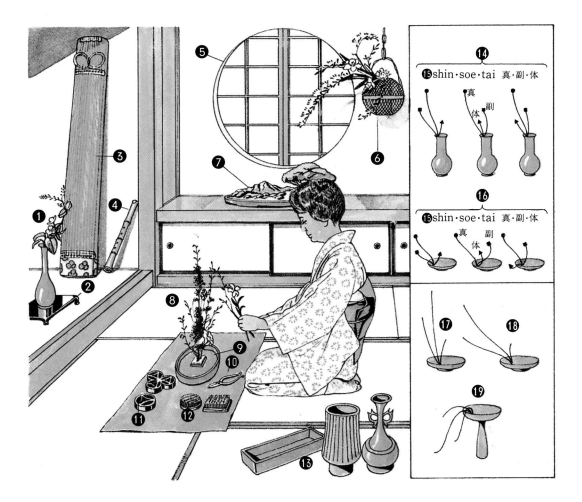

1  **ichirin-zashi:** single-flower vase
2  **kadai:** vase stand
3  **koto:** stringed musical instrument
4  **shakuhachi:** vertical Japanese flute
5  **maru-mado:** round window
6  **tsuri-bana:** ceiling-hanging flower arrangement
7  **bonkei:** miniature landscape
8  **rikka:** standing flower arrangement
9  **suiban:** shallow basin for flowers
10  **hana-basami:** flower scissors

11  **hana-dome:** flower holder
12  **kenzan:** needle-point flower holder
13  **kaki:** any flower container
14  **nageire:** "thrown-in" arrangement
15  **shin soe tai:** Ikenobo school basic arrangments
16  **mori-bana:** "piled-up" arrangement
17  **chokutai:** upright style
18  **shatai:** slanting style
19  **suitai:** hanging style

# YAKIMONO

## Pottery & Ceramics

THROUGHOUT the world, Japanese pottery is prized for its unassuming beauty and elegant simplicity of form and color. The standards of technical excellence and artistic achievement that have elevated Japanese pottery to such distinction have evolved over many hundreds of years. Modern Japanese potters use not only centuries-old techniques from China and Korea but have perpetuated native traditions in combination with European glazes and processes they adapted. Because of this Japan is arguably the pottery center of the world.

In no other country of the world has an esthetic appreciation of ceramics developed to as high a level as in Japan. A foreigner looking at a Bizen vase—rough, misshapen, and covered with rusty splotches—may not be impressed by it. But in Japan, ceramic ware has traditionally been judged not by its outward beauty but by its utility. This utilitarian view was held by the founders of the tea ceremony who chose to use commonplace objects like rice bowls from which to drink the ceremonial tea.

The integral part that pottery began to play in the tea ceremony did much to encourage competition among potters to produce fine quality bowls and other tea utensils. They made ceramic objects for other arts as well: *kabin*, vases for floral arrangements; *koro*, hand-held censers for the incense ceremony; and *suiteki*, the small water container used in calligraphy.

Apart from its importance to the tea ceremony, pottery is so much a part of daily life in Japan that it is difficult to imagine a meal without it. Because tableware is a necessary part of the cuisine, dishes are chosen to blend not only with the food that is put on or in them but with the occasion, the time of day, the atmosphere of the room, and with the season.

The variety in tableware is extraordinary. Ceramic objects range in size from dainty *hashioki* (chopstick rests) and *sakazuki* (saké cups) to medium size plates and bowls, *tokkuri* (sake containers), *dobin* (teapots) and *yunomi* (teacups). The many sizes and shapes the dishes come in—round, oval, square, rectangular, pentagonal, leaf-shaped, fan-shaped, flower-and-vegetable-shaped—lend character and variety to the table.

The way food is served on plates in Japan contrasts with the way it is served in the West and in other Asian countries. Westerners, accustomed to eating from individual large plates supplemented by a few smaller flat plates, are at first amazed at the number of small plates and bowls that are set before each person at a Japanese meal. In China food is served in large bowls or on huge platters and is eaten from small bowls. Meals in Korea are usually served in individual bowls. Flat plates are rarely used.

Although *yakimono* refers to pottery in general, Japanese often distinguish between two basic types of ceramic ware: stoneware and porcelain. *Yakimono* is characterized by a rough appearance, glazed or unglazed. Representative pottery of this type comes Mashiko, Kasama, and Shigaraki. Porcelain objects when held up to the light appear translucent. Arita, Imari, and Nabeshima wares are well known among porcelain fanciers. Stoneware, because of its texture, has few intricate drawings compared to the great number on porcelain ware.

It is inevitable that the process of making ceramic goods is becoming increasingly mechanized. In spite of this trend, the quality and esthetic appeal of the final product are reaching a wider and more appreciative audience.

# NIHONGA

## Japanese Paintings

NIHONGA—a difficult but not impossible concept to define. Broadly considered, it could embrace some fourteen centuries of Japanese painting. Narrowly interpreted, it could refer to the efforts of a few individuals during the early Meiji era, artists led by Okakura Tenshin who sought to create modern schools of Japanese art. But most accurately defined, *nihonga* would refer to *yamato-e* (Japanese-themed paintings of medieval times). For its beginnings in the tenth century marked a key turning point in the history of Japanese-style painting. It was the first of what one critic has called "cyclic alternations between Chinese influences and an aboriginal strain, or between philosophical restraint and a native impulsiveness."

When modern Japanese artists such as Hogai and Taikan determined to revive traditional painting styles, they looked to the two mainstreams of Japanese art, the *yamato-e* and the Kano styles. Both these movements had in turn originated in China.

After some two centuries of highly imitative work, Japanese painting slowly replaced Chinese scenes with familiar Japanese landscapes. During the Heian period, artists produced *shiki-e*, sets of panels or screens on which the four seasons appeared. It was also called *tsukinami-e*, a month-by-month depiction of seasonal changes. *Meisho-e*, another popular form, reproduced famous places of the time.

Painting during the Heian period belonged principally to the upper classes. It was their homes that the characteristic flat color masses of the *yamato-e* graced. Their lives were featured on screens and scrolls, and their customs appeared in literary pieces such as the *Genji Monogatari*. Both for its earlier Heian phase and its final Kamakura period, *yamato-e* produced an artistic chronicle of everyday life.

When *yamato-e's* influence began to undergo a decline, a second wave of Chinese painting came to Japan, this time combined with religious ideas—those of Zen Buddhism. *Suibokuga*, or ink painting reached its zenith in Japan under Sesshu, a Zen priest. However, ink painting became separated from its religious context and a new Japanese school of professional painters emerged. This Kano school, as it was called, accounts for the inspiration that guided the contemporary brush artist, Taikan.

During the Edo period, *yamato-e* reappeared in the highly decorative works of four principal artists from the *Rinpa*, or Korin school. Koetsu, Sotatsu, Kenzan and Korin produced *hekiga* (mural painting), *fusuma-e* (sliding-door painting), and *byobu-e* (folding-screen painting). Color, not ink lines, dominated their works, as did many of the historical themes of old Japan. The next appearance of *yamato-e* came during the late part of the eighteenth century, when *ukiyo-e* (*yamato-e's* offspring) masters began their colorful rendering of everyday Edo life.

Today *nihonga* reflects European, Chinese, and indigenous strains of influence, but maintains traditional feelings for its own sense of beauty. And it is to the *yamato-e* that it owes its spirit of independence. For *yamato-e* was the catalyst for a truly national art—*nihonga*.

# SHODO

## Calligraphy

IN JAPAN, calligraphy (*shodo*) has long been a major art form. Originally the art of writing Chinese characters (*kanji*) was introduced to Japan, together with Buddhism, by Chinese priests who came to Japan and by Japanese who had traveled to China to study. The Chinese writing system was admired not only because it was the vehicle for Buddhist teachings, but also because it was a manifestation of the powerful, charismatic personalities of the priests. Some of the greatest of these priests even had tales and legends built up around their prowess with the brush.

The great Kobo Daishi, a famous monk and scholar in early Japanese history, was said to have on one occasion leapt in the air holding a brush in each hand, a brush gripped in the toes of each foot, and one clenched between his teeth, with which he managed to draw five perfect characters before he touched the ground! Clearly, skill with calligraphy was the stuff of legend.

In some respects writing developed along similar lines in Europe during the Middle Ages. Writing, as well as other forms of learning, was developed and preserved by monks and scholars. Because there was no printing process available, books were copied by hand. For the scribes who did this work, legibility and precision were of great importance. Except in the "illuminated" texts of some prayer books, the work of European calligraphers seldom rose to the level of real art. In Japan *shodo* has always been considered a fine art, akin to painting, a medium through which the artist finds self-expression. Even today calligraphy is exhibited in galleries and displayed in the *tokonoma* (a room's decorative alcove).

Difficulties in adapting Chinese characters for writing the Japanese language led to the development of a Japanese writing system—eventually two syllabaries of *kana* symbols. One of these, *hiragana*, was originally called *onnade*, "woman's hand." Nevertheless, virtually all the great Japanese calligraphers have been men. Great importance is placed on expressing the individual's personality in Japanese calligraphy. In the West, the subject of handwriting analysis is quite popular, and even computers are used in the analysis of a person's handwriting. But typically, judgements about one's personality—as viewed through his or her handwriting—are rather negative in tone. By contrast, expressing one's personality in Japanese calligraphy is seen as a display of skill and refinement.

Japanese study calligraphy to develop their character and to develop a sense of esthetics as well. A foreigner might observe that a Japanese sometimes shows more concern about the appearance than the content of something written. But this attitude fails to appreciate the union of form and content in *shodo*. A powerful verse can be complemented by forceful strokes of the brush, or a poem about butterflies can be written so that one can almost see them fluttering about on the paper.

The foreigner who tries to study Japanese calligraphy may be discouraged by the difficulty of making even the simplest strokes. Yet the expert calligrapher can use large or small brushes with great subtlety and can use them in more than one style of writing.

# Shodo and Sumi-e, the Art of the Brush

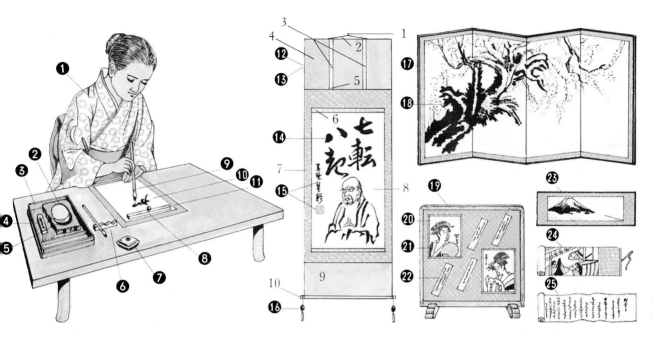

1 **shoka:** professional calligraphy artist

2 **suzuri:** inkstone

3 **suzuri-bako:** box for inkstone and utensils

4 **sumi:** India inkstick

5 **suzuri-no-umi:** hollow in inkstone

6 **fude-oki:** brush rest

7 **suiteki (suichu):** water dropper

8 **bunchin:** paperweight

9 **fude:** brush

10 **hanshi:** calligraphy paper

11 **shita-jiki:** pad underneath paper

12 **kakejiku:** hanging scroll

  1 **makio:** excess hanging string

  2 **kakeo:** string for hanging *kakejiku*

  3 **futai:** ornamental strips at top of artwork

  4 **ten:** top, or upper, area

  5 **tsuyu:** ornamental fringe beneath *futai*

  6 **ichimonji:** accenting borders

7 **chumawashi:** background

8 **honshi:** main section

9 **chi:** bottom, or lower, area

10 **jiku:** spindle

13 **yamato-hyogu:** formal-style scroll

14 **gasan:** verse written on painting

15 **rakkan:** calligrapher's signature or seal

16 **fuchin:** decorative scroll-weights

17 **byobu:** folding screen

18 **sumi-e:** monochrome painting

19 **tsuitate:** low screen

20 **shikishi:** square card for calligraphy

21 **ukiyo-e:** style of woodblock print

22 **tanzaku:** rectangular card for calligraphy

23 **gaku:** framed calligraphy or *sumi-e*

24 **emaki:** illustrated narrative scroll

25 **maki-gami:** rolled calligraphy paper

# *WASHI*

## Japanese Paper

JAPANESE handmade paper, *washi*, is one of the favorite souvenirs bought by foreign visitors in Japan. Many small, useful items are made of *washi*. Purses, stationery and fans are ideal gifts to be taken back home by foreigners worried about the weight of their luggage. More important, a *washi* gift captures the beauty of a traditional Japanese folk art, paper making.

*Washi* has mistakenly been called "rice paper" in the West. Although there actually is such a paper made from a rice-paper plant (*Tetrapanax papyriferus*), as well as other kinds of paper made from grass, hemp, and straw, *washi* is distinctive in its manufacture and its beauty. It is made from the bark of the *kozo* (mulberry) tree and the *mitsumata* and *gampi* trees—both indigenous to Asia—and not from wood chips, as Western-style paper is made.

The bark is first boiled and washed, then is picked through by hand to catch any impurities. When it is clean it is beaten, either by hand or by machine, to separate it into small fibers about 3 to 5 millimeters long. These minute fibers are caught up in a net filter. A viscous liquid obtained from the crushed root of the *tororo aoi* (hollyhock) is vital in the making of *washi*. This liquid is added to water in a wooden box and is adjusted to the correct den-

sity, then the separated fibers are added to the mixture. Above the water is a frame (*keta*) made from one layer of silk screen, closely woven and smooth, and one layer of bamboo, loosely woven and rough. This frame is dipped by hand into the fiber-and-liquid mixture, and a process of picking up and sifting begins. As the fibers are mixed they begin to congeal into a solid sheet of paper. The papermaker can control the weight of the sheet, producing a 10-, 50-, or 100-gram piece. The wet sheet is placed on a thick cloth and pressed with wood. Then it is placed on a board and hung out to dry.

*Washi* is produced throughout Japan, the most famous locations being Gifu, Kochi, and Fukui prefectures. Each kind of *washi*, however, has its own distinctive beauty.

The beauty of *washi* is in its rich texture and in the design formed by the wood fibers in the paper. The kind of paper made of *mitsumata* bark is used for calligraphy and provides the right surface for the thick black ink and brush strokes.

*Washi* lasts hundreds of years. A testament to this is a volume of ancient Japanese art calligraphy, paintings, screens, and woodblock prints that has lasted over the years. Colors endure and even stay bright since the rich *washi* absorbs the natural dyes like *ai* (indigo) and *benibana* (red).

Besides being used for souvenirs and art *washi* plays a very practical role in Japanese daily life. In any bakery or sweet shop one will find cakes wrapped in *washi*. A century ago *washi* served the same purpose that cloth handkerchiefs do today. And the paper for the yen notes used to buy those *washi* souvenirs is made of the same substance. In the home the decorative white window screens (*shoji*), the room dividers (*fusuma*), traditional-style lamps, and even trays are made of *washi* that usually is a mixture of mulberry bark and pulp.

Most amazing of all things made of *washi*, however, is paper clothing. Museums in Japan display examples of old, ceremonial kimono and other garments made of *washi*. These seem as strong as any cloth item today. An umbrella of oiled *washi* will keep the rain away. These lovely *bangasa* typify the Japanese art of combining delicate beauty and functional strength.

# TAKE

## Bamboo

THE ENGLISH word "bamboo" probably came from the Malay language (*bambu*) and it brought with it into English a strong exotic nuance. Though some Americans may nostalgically recall their childhood bamboo fishing pole, to some the very sound of the word may evoke a drumbeat echoing across a humid jungle valley. So when touring the northern countryside in Japan it is rather surprising to see bamboo groves covered with snow; the two do not seem to go together.

But more surprising is the fact that bamboo, an essential part of life in Japan and much of Asia, is one of the most totally useful plants known to mankind. No part of the plant need be wasted and in the East its shoots are eaten, and its stalk is made into everything from eating utensils, musical instruments and fans to brooms, fences and bridges. Its leaves are used to wrap or decorate food. And the whole plant itself is an essential material employed to aesthetic effect in the art of *ikebana* as well as in numerous religious rituals and festivals such as *Tanabata*.

In Japanese bamboo is *take*, a word with a connotation of uprightness and resilience. It bends easily in the wind and even when laden with snow snaps back as soon as the snow begins to melt. Its growth rate is legendary, and observers have measured as much as four feet of growth in a day. Some people claim in all seriousness to have actually seen bamboo grow before their very eyes.

Some 400–500 species (of over 1,000 species worldwide) are found in the temperate and subtropical regions of Japan. The tallest type of bamboo, which the Japanese call *take*, blooms rarely, only once in 10–40 years. One of the largest species, *madake*, grows to a height of 20 meters and provides the material used in the making of poles and *shakuhachi* flutes.

Naturally, plates, baskets, and screens made of bamboo are both light and extremely strong.

Because of the beauty of the material itself, things made of bamboo appear not so much as manufactured products but rather as natural objects molded or fitted into shape. Since bamboo does keep its natural character, it adds a distinctive feeling of warmth and texture to the simplest of everyday things. In the tea ceremony (*chanoyu*) bamboo has a starring role. It is a central building material of the tea house (*chashitsu*). The bamboo scoop for powdered tea (*chashaku*) and bamboo water ladle (*hishaku*) both display bamboo's simple beauty. The tea whisk (*chasen*) is certainly one of the most delicate, intricately made utensils. Some have as many as 120 thin splines. Bamboo chopsticks are also regularly used, and some rough bamboo containers holding simple arrangements of seasonal flowers (*chabana*) date back hundreds of years and are treasured heirlooms.

After living in Japan for a while one comes to notice little things like the fresh flowers arranged in a corner of an office or bank, or the real bamboo leaves (*sasa*) used to decorate a plate of *sushi*. These days many of the traditional uses of bamboo are being taken over by metal or even plastic, with a definite loss of aesthetic appeal. The decorative bamboo leaves are being replaced by a bright green, easily recognizable plastic imitation. Yet somehow the real thing adds a mysterious freshness to *sushi* and a cool, clear accent to food that plastic can never equal.

# NOH & KYOGEN

## Japanese Drama

CONSIDER the apocryphal story of an American visitor to Japan who was lavishly entertained by his Japanese hosts. To let him see as much of Japan as possible, their schedule included a visit to a Noh play. The American sat through the first act with gritted teeth and glazed eyes, and exerted an almost superhuman effort to at least feign polite interest. Then he caught a glimpse of his two Japanese companions—both blissfully asleep! This story says much about this ancient dramatic form which most Japanese willingly consider a "national treasure" but which few have the patience to endure. And even enthusiastic fans are ready to admit that not many people take to Noh on first exposure. Instead, it takes some preparation to study the plots, read the program notes, and to learn to appreciate the music produced by three drums and a flute.

Actually, the word "play" is somewhat misleading when applied to Noh. It is really a blending of recitation, chants, and ritual dancing focusing on Buddhist themes or concepts in which a "moral" or ethical principle is offered to illustrate righteous behavior. Many dramas feature the souls of the dead in speaking roles or include the roles of plants, animals, and other "spirits." And the actors—all roles, even female ones, are played by men—chant their lines in a warbling, "sing-song" cadence.

While the origins of Noh can be traced back 1,000 years to the T'ang Dynasty in China, the traditional Noh drama seen today was developed in the fourteenth century under the patronage of the Ashikaga shogun and remained the chief entertainment of the court and the feudal aristocracy for some 400 years. By the beginning of the eighteenth century, however, Japanese audiences were flocking to see the vastly more popular Kabuki dramas. Although Noh continued to retain some snob appeal and was officially considered the only proper entertainment for samurai and aristocrats, more and more Japanese—even those in high positions—came to regard it as an esoteric, even effete, taste. What is most interesting, perhaps, is that Noh enjoys its present role as an officially protected and encouraged classical art form due to the efforts of Tomomi Iwakura, one of the early Meiji oligarchs. In 1873, following his inspection tour of Europe and America during which he was frequently entertained at operatic performances, Iwakura decided that Noh was akin to grand opera and should be preserved to entertain foreign dignitaries.

There is, however, a different form of dramatic art which is related to the classical Noh play. Called Noh *kyogen*, or more simply, *kyogen* (literally "crazy talk"), the plays feature amusing dialogues—or monologues—about human foibles in everyday life. Performers are frequently seated on the floor and rely simply on witty dialogue, puns, and gestures to keep their audiences laughing uproariously. While the art was developed along with Noh during the fourteenth century, *kyogen* did not at first achieve the same official esteem as its loftier and more elegant cousin. By the Tokugawa period, however, its 300-year heritage gave the tradition-bound shogunate ample reason to encourage *kyogen* over the "immoral" upstart, Kabuki, and Noh flourished. In modern Japan, time and changing tastes have caught up with both Noh and *kyogen*—and even with Kabuki. Audiences for these performances seem to be older and older every year as younger Japanese turn to movies, TV, disco dancing, and a variety of other entertainment forms.

# Noh and *Kyogen* Masks and a Noh Stage

1 **noh-men:** Noh masks
2 **kojo:** mask of old man
3 **chujo:** mask of a nobleman
4 **ko-omote:** mask of a young woman
5 **hannya:** mask of a female demon
6 **kyogen-men:** masks for *kyogen*
7 **buaku:** mask of a demon
8 **usofuki:** comical pouting mask
9 **saru:** mask of a monkey
10 **kitsune:** mask of a fox
11 **hashi-gakari:** bridge-like corridor
12 **koken:** assistant to main actor
13 **shite:** main actor in Noh play

14 **taiko:** drum played with sticks
15 **o-tsuzumi:** large hand-drum
16 **ko-tsuzumi:** small hand-drum
17 **fue:** Japanese flute
18 **ai-kyogen:** *kyogen* actor who performs between acts
19 **waki:** second actor who performs without a mask
20 **tsukuri-mono:** stage setting of Noh play
21 **ko-kata:** child actor
22 **ji-utai:** onstage chorus
23 **kagami-ita:** background panel of Noh stage
24 **noh-butai:** a Noh stage
25 **kensho:** the section for the audience

# KABUKI

## Japanese Drama

WHEN ONE hears the word *kabuki*, formality comes to mind. It recalls the things seen in pictures: colorful costumes, elaborate sets, and exaggerated gestures and face makeup. Naturally, it is easy to assume that Kabuki has always been the classical theater of Japan, just as the Greek theater has been for the West.

Most people are therefore quite surprised to learn about Kabuki's real origins, namely, that the first Kabuki plays were not plays at all, but erotic dances. They were performed by courtesans for male audiences. It is said that the first Kabuki dancer, Okuni, wore a bright red dress, danced wildly, and played the tambourine. Later she wore men's clothes and carried a sword. By playing scenes in which she flirted with a woman she gained enormous popularity with her audiences.

In 1629 the shogunate banned all female performances of Kabuki. Young boys then took the place of women, but these youths too were

forbidden in 1652 to perform. Because the public wanted it, "youth" Kabuki soon reappeared. It returned, however, with several changes. The young boys were forced to shave the hair from the front parts of their heads, like adult males. They were not allowed to sing or dance. Without their youthful hairstyles and erotic dances, they were forced to do nothing but act. In a sense Kabuki became a fine art because of government interference.

By the Genroku era (1688–1704), Kabuki had already become a serious, yet popular, form of theater. Roles and plots became complicated; at the same time dramatic skill was emphasized. It was during this period that Japan's greatest playwright, Monzaemon Chikamatsu, lived. He spent his life developing Kabuki as an art form, and has been called the "Shakespeare of Japan."

A few comparisons can be made between Kabuki in general and Shakespearean drama. In Tokyo, tourists from Japan and abroad visit the Kabuki-za daily. Their tour buses crowd together in the Ginza, loading and unloading passengers. Likewise, tour buses leave London, taking British as well as foreign tourists to Stratford-on-Avon. There, in Shakespeare's home town, his plays are often performed out-of-doors, just as they were during his lifetime.

In England and in Japan the audiences at such performances have much in common. Many are tourists seeking "instant culture." Few of them understand everything that is said onstage, but it does not matter. The spectacle—the sets, the costumes, the music—is enough.

In addition to tourists, there are the more serious playgoers. Kabuki fanatics will see every play every season and sit in the theater for four full hours. During the intermissions, these fans talk continuously, exchanging their opinions of the play and the actors' performances. Their counterparts in the West are the "students of Shakespeare."

But in both places, the tourists dominate. The American crosses the Atlantic on a bargain tour for a "once-in-a-lifetime experience." Many Japanese people not living in Kyoto, Osaka or Tokyo do the same. Often they have won their Kabuki tour in a sales-promotion lottery. For most, it is an experience they will never forget.

# A Performance of the Kabuki Classic *Sukeroku*

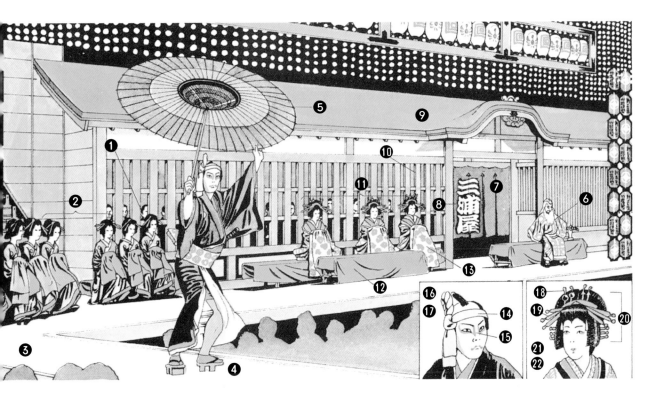

1  **hayashi-kata:** Japanese classical arts musicians

2  **shinzo:** attendant for a high-ranking courtesan

3  **hana-michi:** aisle-stage used for dramatic entrances

4  **mie:** dramatic pose assumed by kabuki actors

5  **ja-no-me gasa:** oil-paper umbrella used in kabuki

6  **Ikyu:** the villain in the kabuki play *Sukeroku*

7  **noren:** curtain hung over the entrance to a shop

8  **yago:** name of a shop, also used for kabuki actors

9  **yukaku:** the part of a city dedicated to brothels

10  **koshi:** latticework window

11  **tayu:** top-rank courtesan, also called an *oiran*

12  **shogi:** a bench

13  **kakae-obi:** kimono sash, tied in front

14  **hachi-maki:** headband

15  **kuma-dori:** makeup that exaggerates kabuki actor's expressions

16  **Sukeroku:** the leading role in the kabuki play of the same name

17  **tachi-yaku:** actor who performs male roles

18  **kanzashi:** long, ornamental hairpin

19  **kogai:** flat, ornamental hairpin

20  **tate-hyogo:** special hairstyle worn only by courtesans

21  **Agemaki:** name of the tayu loved by Sukeroku

22  **oyama:** actor who performs female roles

# BUNRAKU

## Puppet Plays

VERY FEW Westerners who have had the chance to see *bunraku*, the traditional Japanese puppet play, have failed to be impressed by the performance. *Bunraku* is one element of Japanese culture that seems to transcend the language barrier easily. Indeed, within the last two decades, touring *bunraku* companies in the United States, Europe, and Australia were met by very enthusiastic audiences. Despite the ancient and unfamilar themes of the plays, many Westerners were fascinated by the genius of the puppeteers in evoking lifelike moods and emotions simply through manipulating the *bunraku* puppets.

Actually, the dolls used in *bunraku* plays are quite large—sometimes almost one meter in length—and therefore very heavy. Each doll is usually operated by three puppeteers. One handles the head and right arm, another operates the left arm, and the third manipulates the feet. And rather than being hidden from the audience as puppeteers are in the West, *bunraku* operators appear onstage with the dolls. They are dressed in black, and the audience is supposed to ignore their presence. Curiously, after watching the dolls move about the stage for some time, it becomes quite possible to ignore the operators and fully concentrate on the tale at hand, but many viewers stare in awed admiration at the highly intricate, coordinated maneuvers as the three silent figures work together in perfect harmony. Most operators have spent ten years in apprenticeship and practice before actually performing. One famous puppeteer spent his entire career operating the left arm only!

As groups of operators onstage manipulate the *bunraku* dolls to simulate walking, talking, fighting, dancing, and a whole range of gestures and expressions, the story line of the play, or *joruri*, is recited by a group of offstage *dayu*, or readers. Accompanied by *shamisen* music, the readers offer both commentary and dialogue. *Bunraku* plays are not intended for children, however. The themes of tragedy or an occasional comedy are clearly aimed at an adult audience. Many of the stories are surprisingly shocking, and tales of death and suicide are not uncommon at all. The frequently presented historical romantic tales ( *jidaimono*) with five acts, or parts, lasting eight hours, are often cut to about four hours for most performances. Realistic tales (*sewamono*) usually consist of three parts only and are presented in their entirety.

*Bunraku* was created in the early 1600s in the Kansai area and quickly gained many enthusiastic fans. By 1684 regular performances were being scheduled in Osaka by Gidayu Takemoto, considered by many to be the founder of the modern art. While *bunraku* is still enjoyed by many Japanese, like other traditional arts it has lost large numbers of its audience to TV, the theater, movies, and other forms of popular modern entertainment. It now receives national protection and encouragement as an important cultural property, however, and four or five performances are held annually in Osaka and three or four in Tokyo. It is interesting to note that today, as in the past, *bunraku* has been enjoyed by people in the Kansai and western Japan areas much more than by those in Tokyo. It remains, however, a unique Japanese contribution to the art and skills of puppetry. Uniquely Japanese and displaying all the characteristics of a finely honed craft, a typical *bunraku* performance is the product of generations of artists and craftsmen.

# A *Bunraku* Performance, and Puppet Heads

1  **ningyo-tsukai:** puppeteer

2  **omo-zukai:** leader of a trio of puppeteers

3  **de-zukai:** appearance of the main puppeteer

4  **sannin-zukai:** leader of a trio of puppeteers

5  **kurogo:** stage assistants who wear black

6  **ashi-zukai:** puppeteer for the feet

7  **hidari-zukai:** puppeteer for the left hand

8  **hitori-zukai:** solo puppeteer

9  **tesuri:** screens for hiding puppeteers' feet

10  **kashira:** head of a puppet

11  **o-juto:** head of an old man

12  **waka-otoko:** head of a young man

13  **baba:** head of an old woman

14  **waka-onna:** head of a young woman

15  **yuka:** side stage for a narrator/singer

16  **tayu:** narrator/singer

17  **shamisen-hiki:** shamisen player

18  **futo-shamisen:** shamisen with a thick neck

19  **ito:** three strings of a shamisen

20  **sao:** neck of a shamisen

21  **do:** body of a shamisen

22  **bachi:** plectrum for playing the shamisen

23  **kataginu:** stiff, sleeveless jacket

# *HOGAKU*

## Traditional Music

IF WESTERNERS are asked for their first impressions on hearing Hogaku, or traditional Japanese music, most respond by saying, "Well, it certainly is different!" Despite what appears to be a consensus about "unusual," "strange," or even "eerie" sounds, few respondents can agree on exactly what they heard. Some talk about monotonous choral music without instruments; others describe a high-pitched, wavering flute-like instrument played by a man; others speak of a group of drums and stringed instruments producing what they hear as "atonal" sounds. The situation becomes even more confusing when some strongly dispute any claims of "weirdness" and report being fascinated and charmed by highly melodic songs sung to the accompaniment of a mandolin-like instrument. Even accounting for the differences in musical taste, it seems clear that this is another example of the proverbial story about the blind men describing an elephant.

The problem may be that each of these descriptions is correct—as far as it goes. Hogaku is so varied, and includes so many art forms, that many Japanese experts simply give up trying to define it. Instead, they include any Japa-

nese musical forms created prior to the introduction of Western music and instruments in the Meiji Era. This broad classification actually takes in dramatic forms such as Noh and Japanese dancing, neither of which would be considered "music" in the Western sense. And although the Ministry of Education classifies Noh and Gagaku, or Japanese court music, as separate classical art categories in its annual cultural festivals, most scholars see these forms as subdivisions of Hogaku.

Some forms of Hogaku are both familiar and pleasing to Western ears. For example, string instruments such as the *koto, shamisen,* and *biwa,* all of which are played by plucking the strings like a harp or a classical guitar, include among their standard repertories melodies that can be appreciated by people of any culture. At the same time, however, these instruments are used for some forms of musical expression that many Westerners—and a surprising number of Japanese as well—would label esoteric at best. Similarly, some examples of Japanese choral folk music, Minyo, and folk dancing, *minyo odori,* can find appreciative—if not enthusiastic—audiences simply for their exuberant and catchy tunes. Once again, however, many other examples of these arts would seem strange and "nonmusical" to individuals accustomed to standards in keeping with the Western musical tradition.

And one would be safe in assuming that some other forms of Hogaku, such as court music, Buddhist music, music on the five-holed bamboo flute, or *shakuhachi,* and Noh dramatic chants would be so unusual to Western ears that few would manage to listen long enough to discover any redeeming qualities. Actually, this rather negative appraisal of these Hogaku forms is not limited to Western listeners alone; many modern-day Japanese who are well versed in all forms of Western music—from opera to hard rock—frankly describe some Hogaku categories as "dreadful." Despite the dwindling audiences for some forms, Hogaku still manages to attract a small but enthusiastic number of serious students who diligently pursue the long and arduous training necessary to master both the instruments and techniques of Japan's ancient musical tradition.

# HAIKU

## Five-Seven-Five Poems

HAIKU is a literary form that many Westerners are only vaguely familiar with, if at all. Western students of literature are aware of *haiku* as a poetry form, of course, but they rarely can appreciate its simplicity or beauty since they must read the poems in translation.

Scholars are not certain when the first Japanese poem was written, but it probably was in the sixth or seventh century. At first there were long poems that existed along with shorter ones. The longer poems, *choka*, sometimes had between 50 and 100 lines. The important rule was that lines of five and seven syllables must alternate and that the last line must have seven syllables. By the ninth century the shorter form, *tanka*, had become more popular. *Tanka* was composed of five lines with a total of thirty-one syllables in a 5-7-5-7-7 sequence.

During the Heian period, poetry was a part of life in the royal court, where people had time to compose poems daily. Those of high rank were expected to write witty and beautiful poems. In the eleventh century poetry contests were held. These produced *renga:* One person would provide the last two lines of a poem, then another person had to compose the first three lines. When put together, all five lines had to make a meaningful thirty-one-syllable poem. It was from *renga* that *haikai*, the predecessor of *haiku*, was born. *Haikai* consisted of the first three lines of the thirty-one-syllable *renga* poems. *Haikai* become popular during the Edo period. During the Meiji Era this poetry form was modernized and became even more popular. Thus *haiku* came into existence.

What is *haiku?* There are four general rules, although they are not always followed. The first is that the poem must have seventeen syllables in a 5-7-5 sequence. The second is that the poem must make some reference to nature This reference can be an implied allusion instead of a direct statement. The third rule is that the poem must refer to something concrete, not to an abstraction or generalization. And the last rule is that the reference must be to something that exists now, not something from the past.

The aim of *haiku* is to make the reader feel what the writer has felt. Special words and phrases are used as references to nature, to set the tone to provide keys to deeper meanings. The moon, for example, represents autumn and the month of September. Other favorite subjects of *haiku* are flowers, birds, snow, falling leaves, love, and life's brief duration.

There is no Western poetry form that is as strictly defined and structured as *haiku*. The form that comes closest is probably the epigram, a short, terse poem that has one single thought, often expressed in a witty, satirical way. The limerick in English has a structure of five lines with a fixed rhythm and rhyme pattern. But the limerick is usually a light, humorous verse.

*Haiku* is a unique verse form. As such it has attracted the attention and interest of those outside Japan. But in trying to write *haiku* in English, certain problems are encountered. For one thing it is difficult to retain the seventeen-syllable pattern. One reason is that the syllable, as a unit, is defined differently in English and in Japanese. Another is that certain words can be used for punctuation in Japanese *haiku*, but this device cannot be employed in English *haiku*. These problems aside, English *haiku* poets disagree on the use of rhyme and on the necessity of using words and phrases that allude to nature. These difficulties suggest that it may be impossible to limit English *haiku* to the rules that define the original Japanese form.

# SUMO

## Japanese Wrestling

FOREIGNERS seeing sumo for the first time are likely to be shocked by the sight of giant wrestlers competing against wrestlers only half their size. It just does not seem fair. The foreigner, after all, is used to Olympic-style wrestling, where wrestlers are divided into weight classes. In this Greek wrestling tradition, where the object is to pin one's opponent's shoulders to the ground, size makes a big difference. But in sumo the object is entirely different. Sumo takes place on a square mound of dirt elevated about a half meter. On top of this mound is a circle 4.5 meters in diameter. The object in sumo is to push or carry one's opponent out of the ring or to throw him down inside it. In sumo a smaller, more agile wrestler will often out-maneuver larger, clumsier opponents. The techniques of sumo are naturally somewhat different from those of Olympic-style wrestling. First the two sumo wrestlers face each other like two football linebackers and charge each other on cue. Then they slap and push, grab their opponent's belt and lift, trip, or use fancy footwork to put him off balance. After a takedown in Olympic-style wrestling, if neither wrestler can pin his opponent, the match continues for nine minutes. Sumo matches generally last only a few seconds or even less.

Professional all-star wrestling from America is also popular in Japan. Here one can see choking, hair-pulling, kicking, and finger-twisting. In interviews the wrestlers act half-crazed, and after losing a match they are likely to pursue their opponents with folding chairs. The foreigner may thus be surprised to see sumo wrestlers show no more emotion when they win than when they lose. When they are interviewed, the wrestlers are traditionally tight-lipped, and the interviewer has to do almost all the talking himself.

Unlike sports in the West, sumo has a great deal of ritual tied to it. Before the day's top-level matches begin, the wrestlers parade into the ring wearing magnificently embroidered aprons that hang down to their ankles. But when they actually wrestle they wear nothing but a long piece of cloth, wrapped so that it forms a thick belt and a scanty loincloth. The foreigner might worry that this attire could slip off easily. According to the record, however, only one wrestler has ever lost his sash during a match—which he then forfeited automatically. Before each match the two wrestlers perform elaborate rituals of tossing salt to purify the ring, squatting across from each other, and going through a series of standardized motions and glaring at each other. A foreigner who thinks this ritual detracts from the action may prefer to watch an edited replay of the matches on television later. Japanese *sumo* fans, however, enjoy sitting on *zabuton* in the gymnasium all afternoon long, drinking beer or saké while watching the matches.

A *sumo* wrestler has to go through rigorous training. There are matches every two months, all year around. Between these matches, the wrestlers live and train together in stables, where a hierarchy is rigidly observed. The new, younger members are responsible for chores like preparing *chanko*, a fish, meat, vegetable, and tofu stew eaten by the wrestlers. While Western wrestlers work hard at keeping their weight down, the *sumo* wrestlers' training is designed to put as much weight on them as possible. Seeing a few of these enormous men for the first time walking down the street together, a foreigner might wonder if they really are Japanese, huge as they are.

# The Scene at a Sumo Stadium

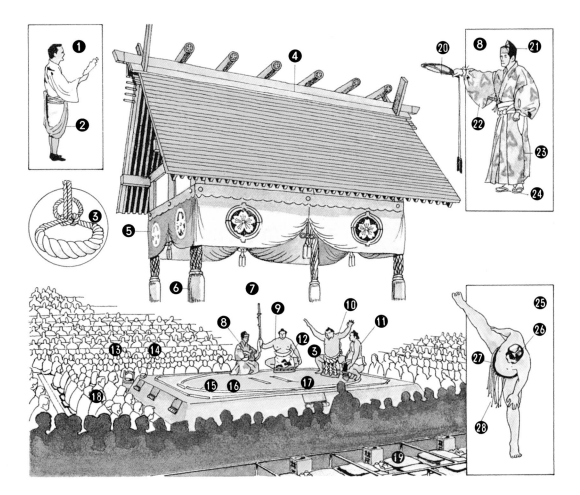

1  **yobidashi:** announcer
2  **tattsuke-bakama:** tapered *hakama* pants
3  **tsuna:** white rope for waist of *yokozuna*
4  **tsuri-yane:** roof above sumo ring
5  **mizuhiki-maku:** narrow curtain for roof
6  **fusa:** decorative tassles for roof
7  **dohyo-iri:** ring-entering ceremony
8  **tate-gyoji:** a sumo referee
9  **tachi-mochi:** sword bearer for *yokozuna*
10  **yokozuna:** sumo grand champion
11  **tsuyu-harai:** wrestler entering ring before *yokozuna*
12  **kesho-mawashi:** emobroidered apron for wresters
13  **mizuoki:** wooden pail for rinsing mouth
14  **shio:** salt

15  **tawara:** straw bag
16  **dohyo:** sumo ring
17  **shikirisen:** marking line
18  **suna-kaburi:** ringside seat
19  **masuseki:** box seat
20  **gunbai uchiwa:** referee's ceremonial fan
21  **eboshi:** headgear worn by referee
22  **hitatare:** referee's ceremonial garment
23  **hakama:** ceremonial skirt-trousers
24  **uwazori:** indoor sandals for top *gyoji*
25  **rikishi:** a sumo wrestler
26  **mage:** topknot hairstyle
27  **mawashi:** long loincloth and belt for wrestlers
28  **sagari:** stringed apron

# JUDO & KARATE

## Hand-to-Hand Fighting

JAPAN has long been noted for its exports, and perhaps the most famous of all are two of its martial arts, judo and karate. Judo, especially, can truly be called an international sport. It has been widely practiced in Western countries for most of the twentieth century, and today there are judo clubs in nearly every major country in the world. Such Japanese words as *waza* (technique), *ki* (spirit), and *kata* (form) are now used in a number of languages.

The international appeal of this sport is such that judo was included in the 1964 and 1972 Olympics. It was significant that the first Open Class Gold Medal was won by a non-Japanese, a Dutch competitor named Anton Geesink. Karate has also developed a steady following abroad. In the U.S., for example, it gained a foothold in the early 1950s and today claims millions of devotees. Interest in karate has been growing rapidly, surviving a temporary wave of kung-fu mania sparked by the films of the late movie idol Bruce Lee in the 1970s.

Despite the widespread familiarity of these martial arts, there are still a number of misconceptions about them in the West. It is generally believed, even today, that Japan is a land of judo and karate fanatics. The truth is, however, that baseball, swimming, and volleyball are today much more popular. Before World War II every Japanese male was forced while at school to study judo or kendo, the art of sword fighting with sticks. This is no longer the case. *Naginata*, another form of stick fighting traditionally learned by women, and *yumi* (archery) have also lost much of their former popularity. Today only a fraction of the Japanese population is skilled in one or more of the country's martial arts.

Moreover, few Westerners realize that the ancient arts of judo and karate are relatively new to the Japanese. Judo, for example, evolved from jujutsu, a form of hand-to-hand fighting originating from the sixteenth century and intended for use by unarmed samurai. Jujutsu was developed for use primarily on the battlefield.

In 1882 a teacher named Jigoro Kano devised a standard version of jujutsu methods and named it *judo*—"the gentle way." Kano's judo consisted of two basic techniques: grappling and throws. Using these a weaker man could take advantage of a stronger opponent's strength and momentum to throw him off balance and, hence, off his feet. Kano changed the emphasis of the discipline from combat, stressing emotional, intellectual, and moral development instead. It was Kano who founded the now world-famous Kodokan school and instituted the belt and degree system of rating.

Foreign karate enthusiasts might be surprised to find that this sport was invented in India by a Buddhist monk, refined in China and later developed in Okinawa. It was not until the 1920s that it became popular in Japan.

If lovers of judo are initially attracted by the gentler aspects of the sport, karate fans are invariably taken with the flashier, more violent side of the "art of the empty hand." New converts are particularly impressed with the ability of karate masters to smash bricks, boards, and bottles with the edge of the palm. They are eager to learn how to make their own fists, elbows, and feet worthy of being called "deadly weapons."

Students of both disciplines, however, eventually discover one thing: the ultimate reward for their efforts is the spiritual joy of attaining a oneness of mind and body.

# KENDO & KYUDO

## Japanese Fencing & Archery

THE CHARACTER *do*, meaning "road" or "way," is used in the Japanese words for fencing (kendo) and archery (*kyudo*). The meaning of the character changed, however, in the transition from the Edo period to the Meiji Era. Through the Edo period the "way" of the sword and bow were considered practical skills.

With the Meiji Restoration, however, the *samurai* cut their hair, and the swords they once carried were prohibited by law. The "way" of the sword, like that of the bow, was no longer a practical skill. It became, instead, a discipline, a way of self-mastery that was strengthened through meditation. Training in kendo is based on a variety of movements that combine attack and defence, called *waza*. These include such elements as footwork, cuts and thrusts, and parrying.

Before any practice of kendo, the participant kneels quietly (*seiza*) and tries to forget any daily worries. Head and heart become one, and with this attitude the match is approached. Eye contact is essential for understanding an opponent's course of action. Will the opponent strike at head (*men*), hand (*kote*), or body (*do*)? Or is his concentration so weak that it would allow for a thrust at his throat (*tsuki*)? The moment one's guard is down the opponent strikes and the point is lost.

In contrast to the competition and accuracy of kendo, kyudo is a graceful, stylized ceremony. Form and economy of movement are all-important, the target being secondary. As in kendo, a short period of meditation is done before any practice.

The most fascinating part of both kendo and kyudo for the foreign spectator is the dramatic spectacle of the uniforms and the equipment. The basic jacket (*gi*) is handmade and stitched in *sashiko* design, heavier for kendo, lighter for kyudo. The black skirtlike pants are *hakama*. Over these the fencer wears a black helmet and mask (*men*), which is quite long and covers the neck. There is also a chestplate (*do*) made of hard leather and a long bamboo staff (*shinai*).

The bow (*yumi*) used in kyudo is taller than the archer, thus adding to the dramatic effect of the ceremony. The arrows (*ya*) are made of bamboo. The archer wears a special glove since the arrow is shot from the right, causing the bow to twist to the left. Great skill is required to hold the bow when it recoils.

In Western fencing the arms are open at the sides of the body and come across to parry and lunge. In archery the bull's-eye is all-important. But in kendo and kyudo the power comes from the middle of the torso, from within (*ki*). The torso is closed and protected by the arms, since an opening could invite a strike by the opponent. According to devotees, it is this concentration and flow of ki energy that lends such grace to kyudo.

Western sports are far more standardized in comparison to kendo and kyudo, and there are few special schools or styles to devote oneself to. But in Japan the school, style, and instructor (*sensei*) are very important. Understanding this approach is sometimes difficult for foreigners whose independent nature may be viewed by the Japanese *sensei* or students as disloyalty.

The essence of any discipline is contained in the proverb, *Aite ni katsu yori, onore ni kate*—which translates approximately as "Try not to beat your opponent; try, instead, to win over yourself."

# GEISHA

## The Art People

THE word *geisha* (literally "art people") is well known in the West, and the image of the large hairpiece, heavy makeup, and elaborate kimono are familiar. The real meaning of geisha, however, is usually misunderstood by foreigners, many of whom think a geisha is akin to a prostitute. Although the line separating geisha and prostitutes is a thin one in some situations, the concept of geisha has a long and honorable history. Dancing girls in the thirteenth century, during the Kamakura period, were called *shirabyoshi* (literally "white rhythm"), probably in reference to the heavy white makeup they used.

At that time there was no clear distinction between artists and prostitutes. During the Edo period, however, this concept changed. The name geisha was adopted to designate a professional entertainer at a licensed establishment. These artists were not supposed to be in competition with courtesans. They grew up in a special world, surrounded by other women devoted to traditional Japanese song, dance, and music.

Modern women seeking to become geisha must still take lessons in a number of traditional

arts, and most learn to play the *shamisen* (a three-stringed banjo-like instrument), the *tsutsumi* (a small drum played on the shoulder), and the *kodaiko* (a small drum played with wooden sticks); some even study English. In Kyoto there are apprentice geisha called *maiko* (dancing girls). In earlier times, prior to the current compulsory education law that requires everyone to attend middle school, they would have started as young as thirteen but even so these girls are young, between sixteen and twenty years old. Like other geisha they are trained in the traditional arts of entertainment.

The appearance of a geisha is fascinating to the Western eye. To some she represents the old traditional beauty of Japanese women, and to some she is a garish circus clown. Her hairstyle is fashioned after the leaf of the gingko tree (*icho*) and has many ornamental hairpins (*kanzashi*) inserted in the top knot. Her lips are painted red, and the rest of her face is powdered white with a slight accent at the eyes. The white face color has been a traditional symbol of beauty in Japan for centuries. Many feel that white symbolizes the willingness of the geisha to be "dyed" to any color her audience desires. She is supposed to be sensitive in all respects to the entertainment of those to whom, strictly speaking, she sells her art. A goal for many is to eventually own their own restaurant or bar, where they can employ the talents they've spent a lifetime developing.

A geisha's fee can be very expensive, depending on her rank. The *okiya*, or agency, managing the geisha may take a cut of the fee, so this tends to increase the price. Some restaurants employ *nakai*, a status between that of waitress and geisha, for customers on smaller budgets.

A geisha party is a luxury few people can indulge in. They are strictly for the upper management class, executives and politicians. These parties are occasionally used as favors, and—depending on the class of the geisha— the cost per person can start at 50,000 yen. If they do not have an interest in traditional music and dance, Japanese and foreigners alike could find a geisha party a bit formal or even boring. And considering the cost, it makes the local bar seem even more inviting.

# PART THREE

# Recreation
# and Leisure

# GO & SHOGI

## Japanese Board Games

BOTH GO and *shogi* are games that require the power of concentration and an adept mind. These games have been played by Japanese for hundreds of years, and the interest continues today. Many people avidly read books on *go* and *shogi*, and they read articles in newspapers daily to improve their playing skills in much the same way that Westerners do with chess and bridge.

In *go* two players alternately put their stones on any unoccupied intersection on the board. There are 361 of these intersections. The stones are all the same shape and are distinguished by their color—black or white. The black player always goes first, unless more than two handicap stones have been placed on the board. If the abilities of the two players are unequal, the weaker player is allowed to place extra handicap stones on the board before play begins. A weaker player's handicap is usually from two to nine of these prepositioned stones, although even more of them may be allowed.

A stone that has been played cannot be moved unless it is captured. The rules for playing are not very complicated and, generally, if a stone or several stones are surrounded by the enemy's stones, they are considered captured and are removed from the board. Each prisoner

or point within an enclosure (as determined by the number of intersections within a territory) counts as one point. The advantage of the opening move has been determined as five points; thus, if the players' abilities are the same at the outset of the game, the black player must finish with at least six points more than the white player to be the winner. In Western chess no provision is included to compensate for the opening-move advantage.

*Shogi* originated in India, and from there it moved to China, Korea, and finally to Japan; the Indian original was the same game that became chess in the West. The *shogi* board has 81 squares while the Western chessboard has only 64. In *shogi* both the board and the pieces are natural wood, not colored. There are eight kinds of pieces, with their names written on them. The pieces are placed so that they point in the direction in which they are moving across the board. The player can change the power of four of the pieces (*gin*, *keima*, *kyosha*, and *fu*) once they cross the opponent's third row or "promotion" line. At that point the pieces are turned over and they take on the power of *kin*, the "gold" piece. Two other pieces, *kaku* and *hisha*, can be strengthened in the same manner, although they do not assume the same power as *kin*. In chess only the pawn can change power, and then only when it has reached the opponent's back row.

The truly distinctive feature of *shogi* is that a captured piece becomes the property of the capturing side and the piece can be returned to the board for that side's use. At any time, instead of making a move, a player can drop one of these pieces on any vacant square. This gives *shogi* a peculiar excitement because the players must be very much aware of the strategic advantage that one effective drop of a captured piece can have on a game.

Both *shogi* and *go* attract foreign players in Japan. Because *shogi* more closely resembles chess, it usually is mastered quickly by Western enthusiasts. On the other hand *go*, while generally regarded as the more complicated of the two games, has many more adult players and clubs to play in, thus presenting the foreigner with a greater number of opponents to play against.

# An Official *Shogi* Match, and *Go* and *Shogi* Equipment

**SHOGI**

1. **kishi:** professional *shogi* or *go* player
2. **sente:** player with the first move
3. **kiroku-gakari:** game recorder
4. **tachiai:** witness for an official game
5. **gote:** player who moves second
6. **komadai:** stand for captured pieces
7. **mochi-goma:** captured piece
8. **shogi-ban:** *shogi* board
9. **koma:** *shogi* piece
10. **sensu:** folding fan

11. **zabuton:** tatami floor cushion
12. **kyosoku:** armrest (now rare)
13. **koma-ire:** box for *shogi* pieces
14. **memori:** lines on the board
15. **masame:** vertical grain in the wood

**GO**

16. **goban:** *go* board
17. **tengen:** the center intersection on the board
18. **hoshi:** marked point for handicapping
19. **goishi:** the black and white stones used in *go*
20. **goke:** round container for *goishi*

# *JANKEN*

## Hand Games

JANKEN is a popular game among Japanese children. They use the game as a way to decide who will be counted "out" or who will be eliminated, in much the same way American children play "Eeny, meeny, miney mo." *Janken* is a variation on the *ken* (fist) games that were introduced from China during the seventeenth century, historians say. The games first became popular in Nagasaki drinking places. Eventually variations on the *ken* games developed and spread throughout the country. *Janken* was one of those variations.

In the game, a fist means "rock"; the index and middle fingers, parted and extended, mean "scissors"; and an open hand means "paper." The idea is that rock breaks scissors, scissors cut paper, and paper wraps rock. If, for example, one player shows "paper" and the other shows "scissors," the one showing scissors wins. Japanese players call out *jan ken pon* to set the rhythm of the game.

In America some children know and play the game, but they do not call out any special words as they play. The exception is in Hawaii, where children say *Jan kenuh po, I kenuh show*—derived from the Japanese *aiko de sho*, to mean "I can show you" in Hawaiian English. While the basic game is known in the West, its Japanese variations are not. One of the ways to play, for example, is to have one person be the leader, with any number of additional players. Those who do not show what the leader shows, no matter what it is, lose. *Janken* can also be played with one's legs. Legs together is "rock," legs spread is "paper," and one leg forward and one leg back is "scissors." This is often combined with a word game in which players must say words like *guu* for "rock," *choki* for "scissors," and *paa* for "paper." One player might say *gunkan* (warship) with legs together, *chimbotsu* (sink) with one leg forward and one back, and *haretsu* (explosion) with legs spread.

One reason for the continued popularity of *janken* is that it can be played anywhere, at anytime—on the subway, in the street, on the playground, wherever two or more people congregate. It requires no preparation or equipment, and there are no time restrictions.

*Janken* is, of course, more than just a game; it is a handy arbiter that can be used by adults or children. People all over the world use similar ways of deciding who wins and who loses, who goes and who stays. Americans would flip a coin or draw straws. The children would use the chant: "Eeny, meeny, miney, mo; Catch a tiger by the toe; If he hollers, let him go; Eeny, meeny, miney, mo." For this little game, the leader points to a different person as each word is said, and the last person pointed to is the one chosen. In Italy there is a game called *morra* that resembles *janken*—at least from a distance. The players extend their fingers and call out numbers when they play. *Morra* usually is played by men when they are drinking. Its derivation is uncertain; but, like *janken*, it may have originated in China. However, because *morra* is normally used for gambling, it has been declared illegal.

Foreigners who play *janken* in Japan sometimes feel that for some reason they are at a disadvantage. They are often heard to claim that they lose more than their fair share of the time. To them it seems there must be some kind of skill or even mind reading involved in the game. But they probably are the same people who would claim that a penny, when tossed, is more apt to come up showing "heads" than "tails."

# ORIGAMI

## Paper Folding

CHRISTMAS shoppers along Manhattan's Fifth Avenue have been treated to fantastic displays over the years: trees, Santas and angels, all done in lights, run for blocks. But the most unusual holiday scene ever noted there was in the window of a Japanese airline's office. The familiar Christmas sights were there, with the manger in Bethlehem, the Holy Family, the Wise Men and their camels, and the multitude of angels, all were included. But these figures were made exclusively of folded paper, without the use of scissors or paste. Origami, the art of folding paper into beautiful and useful shapes, is a Japanese tradition that is becoming more and more popular in the West.

Folding things is an ever-present activity in Japanese life, from the use of kimono, *furoshiki* (wrapping cloths), futon sleeping mats and even gift envelopes. In fact, the art of folding paper holds an important role in formal Japanese etiquette. There are dozens of ways to fold wrapping paper for gifts, and at weddings and funerals the male and female butterflies that are seen on saké bottles are often exquisitely folded paper ornaments.

Folding paper has its history in ancient times, in ceremonies performed in the court and in shrines. At that time paper was very expensive, and only the nobility could indulge in the ritual of paper folding. Later, in the Edo period, origami developed into an art form as well as an entertainment, with such origami as *senbazuru* (a thousand cranes). This development was closely connected with new techniques in cutting, dyeing, and folding paper in tandem with improvements in the process of making *washi*, handmade paper. But it was not until the turn of the century that, with the availability of cheaper machine-made paper, everyone began to have access to origami. Over the next several decades origami patterns for some 150 standard figures were developed. At this time it was introduced into the primary grades of the Japanese school system under the rationale that paper play would develop logical thinking (especially in mathematics), imagination, creativity, and manual dexterity in children. Today, the use of origami is still a favored educational approach for teaching the relationship between a plane and a solid.

Another argument for origami is that it helps develop an appreciation for another form of beauty that is a departure from traditional Japanese art. In comparison to *shodo* (calligraphy) or raising *bonsai* (dwarf trees), for instance, origami is a precise, symmetrical art with sharp angles and straight lines. Like other forms of creative arts, however, it has a certain subjectivity about it that allows for individual expression. Two origami artists may follow the same steps for making a mask but the end results will be different and will reflect the artists' differing emotions, personalities, and knowledge of the subject.

American interest in origami began in the 1920s when an ethnographer published a book in English about this uniquely Japanese art. He was especially fascinated by the ability of young children to create numerous objects by folding paper. Origami cast its spell over Europe, too. Among the enthusiasts was the Spanish philosopher Unamuno. The limitless variety of shapes and materials appeals to Americans and Europeans alike, who have used bright origami paper, newspaper, *washi*, and even currency for their creations. And there could be an unusual gift: an origami Christmas angel with Benjamin Franklin's face on a $100 bill.

# Common Japanese Games and Toys

1  **origami:** art of folding paper into shapes
2  **ori-zuru:** crane made of folded paper
3  **semba-zuru:** string of 1,000 folded paper cranes
4  **sugoroku:** Japanese version of parcheesi
5  **ayatori:** Japanese-style cat's cradle
6  **o-tedama:** small beanbags for throwing
7  **niramekko:** staring game, the loser laughs first
8  **iroha-garuta:** card game based on the Japanese syllabary
9  **tako-age:** kite flying
10 **fukuwarai:** blindfolded player tries to draw a face
11 **take-uma:** bamboo stilts

12 **take-tombo:** spinning propeller toy
13 **janken:** the "paper-scissors-rock" game
14 **bei-goma:** fighting tops
15 **koma-mawashi:** top spinning
16 **yakko-dako:** kite painted with a feudal footman
17 **hane:** shuttlecock used for *hanetsuki*
18 **hane-tsuki:** battledore game, like badminton
19 **hago-ita:** paddle or battledore for *hanetsuki*
20 **menko:** throwing-card game
21 **mama-goto:** playing house
22 **goza:** straw mat used for playing, picnics, etc.

# HANAFUDA

## Flower Cards

IF YOU ask a Japanese to name the most popular card games in the country, he might pick the Western games of bridge or poker as his first guess and the Japanese game of *hanafuda* as his second. Although probably not as widely played as they are in the West, bridge and poker have gained increasing numbers of enthusiasts within the last several decades. *Hanafuda* is a game that most Japanese know how to play, and some—especially gamblers—play it fairly often. A fact that surprises many of its devoted fans, however, is that *hanafuda* was not a Japanese invention at all. Like its later counterpart, bridge, *hanafuda* was actually a Western import. But it has become so much a part of the culture that most Japanese think of it as their own.

Known variously as *hanafuda, hanagaruta,* or *hanaawase,* the "flower card" game was first introduced to Japan in the late sixteenth century by Dutch traders at Nagasaki. The exciting and fast-paced game caught on very quickly, and local craftsmen were soon making Japanese versions of the cards. Within 100 years *hanafuda* parlors could be found throughout the country; the game was played in tea houses, *machiai,* and other places where people gathered for relaxation.

Although *hanafuda* underwent a number of changes and regional variations in the following centuries, it still takes both skill and some luck to win. The object is to take as many two-card tricks as possible by matching a card in one's hand with one of the same suit turned up on the table. Unlike a bridge deck, the forty-eight-card *hanafuda* deck consists of twelve four-card suits. These suits feature flowers or flowering trees, one for each month of the year. Because the cards in a suit have different point values, however, scoring can be very complicated. It is made even trickier because certain low-card combinations are worth more than some high cards. With the fast pace at which the game progresses, it is clear that playing for money could never be a sport for the weak at heart.

Soon after it was introduced, *hanafuda* became linked with gambling and attracted criminal elements. For this reason the Tokugawa shogunate issued several warnings about wasting time in "frivolous" activities and then finally prohibited the game altogether. The edicts were not very successful, though they were repeated with almost predictable regularity in the years that followed. One final attempt to stamp out the game was made in 1830, when the manufacture, sale, or possession of *hanafuda* was outlawed. Even this measure failed, and the new Meiji government finally gave up trying to eliminate an activity that had become firmly implanted in Japanese life and culture. Today *hanafuda* is like poker in most parts of the United States: recreational games are permitted, although betting, even in penny-ante games, is technically illegal. Of course there are those who cannot resist playing for big stakes. Every year the newspapers report at least half a dozen cases in which police raided a secret *hanafuda* parlor and arrested the players.

Actually, it seems that changing lifestyles, the coming of TV, and the development of other leisure activities have accomplished what government regulations were never able to do. While *hanafuda* is still enjoyed by many people, it is gradually losing ground to other pursuits. Now it is most frequently found as a family activity during the holiday seasons, especially at New Year's.

# PACHINKO

## Japanese Pinball Game

PACHINKO, a vertical pinball game, is said to have originated in Nagoya during the bleak days after World War II. It is not difficult to imagine why Japanese flocked to the glittering noisy shops to spend hours feeding metal balls into the machines. A winner could exchange the balls for cigarettes, candy, and a variety of other goods that were hard to come by in those days. Since that time pachinko has grown into one of the most popular forms of personal entertainment. As of 1996 there were nearly thirty million avid players across the country. Why it continues to attract so many Japanese every day is another question.

It is possible to compare pachinko to the slot machines of Las Vegas which cater to the same kind of addicts, require the same kind of mechanical ritual to play, and are surrounded by the same kinds of superstitions involving "lucky" machines and "lucky" days. But pachinko, from a strictly legal point of view, is not a form of gambling. Though one pays for the metal balls, it is more like borrowing since the balls one wins are exchanged for goods. However, leaving these legal niceties aside, the Japanese game is not confined to one or two

special places but can be played anywhere in Japan, near almost any train station, in shops often lined up four or five in a row.

Though the element of chance and the various prizes one can win are part of the lure of the game, it is probably the place itself, the pachinko parlor, that first attracts the curious visitor. Hundreds of multicolored electric and neon lights rival the largest advertising billboards as visual attractions. Yet the exterior merely hints at the sensory experience that lies within.

Pachinko takes its name from *pachin*, the sound the ball makes as it ricochets through the machine. Multiply one *pachin* by thousands of balls rushing through hundreds of machines and you have quite a din. But add the ever-present John Philip Sousa-style martial music played at eardrum-shattering volume and you have an auditory environment that even the most hardened riveter would find intolerable. Yet the patrons, like monks lost in meditation, seem oblivious to the racket. A psychologist might describe the condition as sensory overload: overwhelmed, the mind stops its normal functions and all that is left is the one circuit that connects the thumb, holding the firing knob, to the eye following the bouncing ball. It must be this kind of hypnotic experience that the real pachinko addict seeks time after time.

The latest automatic machines relieve the player even of the necessity of moving his thumb; he merely turns a knob to fire the balls. Other recent improvements include TV sets placed in the center of the machine itself and shops that look more like gaudy hotel lobbies with chandeliers, mirrors on the walls, and attendants at a front desk.

The popularity of the most recent challenge to pachinko's supremacy, the arcades filled with video games, has been unable to overtake pachinko's number-one spot, and it is easy to understand why. Though the sound of a "hit" produces a hair-raising burst of electronic noise, a video-screen image can hardly compare to the colorful face of the pachinko machine with its sizzling yellow and chartreuse designs, And of course a video game eats up 100-yen coins and gives the player nothing in return but an occasional high score.

# ONSEN

## Hot Springs

WHEN ASKED to offer their idea of an ideal holiday trip, many Japanese, especially those of the older generation, are likely to mention a quiet inn in one of Japan's numerous hot-spring resort areas. Resting in the soothing—and reputedly therapeutic—mineral waters, the traveler forgets the cares and tensions of daily life.

In ancient times the Romans built magnificent baths throughout their empire and took great pleasure in the relaxing effects of the hot water and steam. Perhaps we could also say that bathing devotees are Japanese about their bath. Despite the rise of such activities as skiing and mountain climbing, *onsen* remain an important feature of Japanese tourism.

Many Japanese would undoubtedly agree with the statement that their country is, more than any other, the "land of hot springs." For one thing, because of the geological history of these volcanic islands, Japan has an exceptionally large number of hot springs. Yet another factor is undoubtedly the history of the Japanese people themselves, for whom *onsen* have been an inherent part of a long cultural heritage. Washing with water as a purification rite (*misogi*) is a central element of Shinto religion. The eighth-century *Fudoki* reports that as part of the rite of delivering felicitous messages to the emperor the priestly aristocrats of Izumo would bathe in hot springs.

Of course *onsen* have also been popular for recreational purposes as well. A measure of their importance is the fact that until the end of the Edo period *onsen* were classified according to a number of categories based on social position: There were, for example, *shijinto* for samurai and *choninto* for commoners. Today money, leisure, and personal preference are more likely to determine an *onsen's* clientele.

In eighteenth- and nineteenth-century Europe, hot-spring resorts were a favorite gathering place of the wealthy and aristocratic. The word "spa," now commonly used to translate *onsen*, was originally the name of a hot-spring resort in Belgium. But the European appreciation of hot springs hardly compares to that of Japan. The magnificent center built by the Romans in Bath, England, the site of the country's only hot springs, was destroyed by Saxon invaders and then left neglected until the eighteenth century.

The alleged health benefits of hot-spring bathing have long been a major reason for their popularity. The actual physical benefit is still a subject of controversy, but for those who suffer from tension and insomnia, the soothing effects of both the water and the relaxed atmosphere can hardly be disputed. Karl Marx is known to have traveled on several occasions to a continental spa to lose weight and otherwise try to undo the effects of his rather unhealthy life.

For foreigners in Japan, *onsen* may suggest the romantic setting of Yasunari Kawabata's *Yukiguni*, translated into English by Edward Seidensticker as *Snow Country*. Though a traveler may still find adventure suitable for what Seidensticker calls the "unaccompanied gentleman," the most exotic aspect of a modern *onsen* for the foreign visitor is more likely to be the temperature of the water, which is several degrees above what most Europeans and Americans are accustomed to. Yet for those who do get used to the water, Japanese hot springs are considerable sources of enjoyment. Like the Finnish *sauna*, they are cultural institutions which people of many countries, regardless of language, can come to appreciate.

# RYOKAN

## Japanese Inns

ALTHOUGH it is undoubtedly true that the charm of Japanese inns (*ryokan*) is quickly disappearing because of their rising prices and gradual Westernization, international visitors still find them a refreshing change from Western-style hotels.

One of the most unusual aspects of the *ryokan* experience for a tourist has to do with bathing. First time visitors are surprised to find clean Japanese loungewear (*yukata*) folded neatly in the closet. If one leaves the room between 5:00 and 6:00 P.M., one should expect to see Japanese guests wearing only slippers and *yukata* and carrying bathtowels. This, of course, is because Japanese like to relax before dinner, and the quickest way to do this is to soak in a nice hot tub. Not knowing this, many tourists are slightly embarrassed when their maid encourages them to bathe. Many foreigners think of bathing as a necessity and not necessarily a pleasurable experience. Personal hygiene, to many, is a private matter.

An aspect of *ryokan* life that is appealing to many is the peace and quiet that can be found. It is a luxury to be served in one's room, but it is an even greater luxury to be served by a highly professional and pleasant woman dressed in a beautiful kimono. The beauty of a traditional Japanese table setting is truly a feast for the eyes and often pleases tourists so much that they may even stop to take pictures of the dinner before beginning to eat. The relaxed pace of service is also bound to be appreciated by everyone except the most time-conscious or sleepy foreign guests.

The dining area and sleeping area in a *ryokan* room are the same. After dinner the table is simply cleared and moved aside, and the bedding is laid out on the floor. Some foreigners find it difficult to adjust to eating meals and sleeping in the same part of the room. Of course in Western hotels guests may have their dinner in their room, but usually the table is some distance from the bed. And although many people would not hesitate to have breakfast in bed, few would have dinner that way.

For those who enjoy the relaxing, romantic appeal of dining in their rooms, Japanese inns are ideal. Since both breakfast and dinner are included in the room charge, *ryokan* are very convenient as well. For people who like to eat at different times and in different kinds of restaurants, however, *ryokan* can be expensive. For meals that are not eaten, the *ryokan* usually allows only a small discount.

Americans in particular are often unpleasantly surprised at checkout time when they are asked to pay their bill. Usually they have asked about room rates before checking in. The price they were quoted, however, probably did not include the standard 10- or 15-percent service charge. Giving tips to hotel staff members is a habit for an American, but when tipping at home the customer always has the option of deciding how much to give. The amount given is based upon a subjective opinion of the quality of service one has received. With a fixed service charge, however, this decision-making privilege is taken away.

For every visitor who complains about service charges, however, there are many more who prefer the Japanese system. These people are happy that they do not have to think about money every time a hotel employee enters the room or performs some special service. These kinds of travelers go back home thinking that tipping should be abolished in their native countries.

# PART FOUR

# Cuisine and Diet

食

# NIHON RYORI

## Japanese Cuisine

WESTERNERS who come to Japan often find that Japanese food is not what they had expected. Although in recent years Japanese restaurants have become more common in the West, tourists are not prepared for the "real" Japanese food they encounter once they are here. One reason for this is that most foreigners associate Japanese food with dishes that are not considered traditional fare by the Japanese themselves. Sukiyaki, for instance, is relatively new to Japan, and tempura was introduced by the Portuguese in the sixteenth century. *Teriyaki*, cooked and served in many Japanese restaurants in the West, is seldom eaten in Japan.

The eclectic eating habits of modern Japan include foods from many parts of the world, and this variety is reflected in homes and restaurants all over the country. But real *nihon ryori* is made up of foods that often are not familiar to the Westerner. There is a great preponderance of food from the sea, with an almost total absence of meat. This reliance on the sea as a source of food is quite natural for an island nation like Japan, especially since there is very little land available for raising cattle. Japanese did not begin eating beef and pork until the Meiji period, relatively late in their history.

Putting questions of taste aside for a moment, it is impossible to deny that Japanese cuisine is almost universally regarded as the most beautiful in the world. The careful arrangement of the food has to do with the great concern that Japanese have for design and order. With the serving of food, nothing is left to chance. Food is served in individual lacquer or china dishes that are chosen for their shape and color to suit the food that goes into them. The desired combination of colors and textures is also a factor in choosing the food itself.

The serving of Japanese food is a study in contrasts. Some foods like raw fish will be served on ice in the same meal with hot dishes such as soup. *Daikon oroshi* (grated radish) will be served to complement certain hot foods while green *wasabi* (horseradish) will accompany such cold foods as *sashimi*. Both sweet and sour dishes may be served in the same meal. And additional contrasts are often provided by serving Japanese foods with coarse textures alongside those like raw abalone—however repulsed some Westerners may be by these slick, rubbery textures.

Pieces of pickled radish or eggplant may be added for just the right touches of color. And when several pieces of food are to be placed on one dish, the total effect of the combination must be considered, much the same as in flower arranging. Flowers themselves are often placed in arrangements of food, as are leaves, carved vegetables, and pieces of paper that have been specially cut or folded. These adornments may reflect the seasons—cherry blossoms in spring, paper snowflakes in winter.

Connoisseurs of Japanese cuisine describe it as "delicate" and "subtly complex." They say that because the food is so fresh and its natural taste is so good, no sauces or seasonings are necessary or even desirable. To the non-Japanese palate, accustomed to more spices, such food often seems bland or even tasteless.

But traditional Japanese food does not attempt to make dramatic appeals and displays to appetite and taste alone. Just as the tea ceremony is concerned with much more than the mere drinking of tea, *nihon ryori* is prepared and served to provide a feast for the eyes and the spirit as well as the body.

# Common and Traditional Japanese Foods

1  **zaru-soba:** buckwheat noodles on a bamboo rack

2  **kake-soba:** buckwheat noodles in hot broth

3  **kake-udon:** white noodles made of flour

4  **kishimen:** flat, wheat flour noodles

5  **nabeyaki-udon:** pot-boiled udon

6  **nigiri-zushi:** rice blocks topped with fish

7  **chirashi-zushi:** rice with fish and other toppings

8  **nori-maki:** stuffed rice rolled in laver

9  **oshi-zushi:** blocks of pressed sushi

10  **chakin-zushi:** egg-wrapped sushi

11  **inari-zushi:** rice ball wrapped in bean curd

12  **sashimi:** sliced, raw fish

13  **sukiyaki:** thin-sliced been cooked in broth

14  **shioyaki:** fish broiled with salt

15  **chiri-nabe:** fish stew boiled at the table

16  **yu-dofu:** cubes of soybean curd

17  **tempura:** deep-fried seafood and vegetables

18  **kaba-yaki:** eel dipped in sauce and broiled

19  **yakitori:** charcoal-grilled chicken

20  **oden:** an assortment of simmering foods

21  **su-no-mono:** vinegared vegatables and seaweed

22  **chawan-mushi:** steamed egg custard

23  **saké:** rice wine

24  **chazuke:** rice with tea

25  **onigiri:** rice ball with various fillings

26  **shinko:** pickled vegetables

27  **sui-mono:** clear soup of fish or chicken

# WAGASHI

## Japanese Confectionery

WITH CANDY, as with so much in modern Japan, Western exists side by side with Japanese. Although it is as distinctively Japanese as the word *wagashi* would suggest, Japanese sweets are the product of a variety of foreign influences. First in the Nara period, as trade with China began to flourish, superior Chinese sweets greatly influenced the Japanese version. At the same time, tea, and sugar were introduced to Japan; but sugar remained a rare commodity that only the court and social elite could afford. In Europe, too, sugar was for a long time a rare item, sold as a drug in apothecaries where it sometimes was mixed with bitter ingredients to disguise their taste. Large quantities of sugar were not found in Europe until after the discovery of sugar cane in New World. In Japan, with the influence of Zen and the tea ceremony, confections of superior taste and form were developed, notably in Kyoto. But it was not until the Edo period that confectionery in its modern form became popular among Japanese.

In the mid-sixteenth century, European missionaries brought Western confectionery to Japan and showed the Japanese entirely new ways to use flour, sugar, and eggs in cakes and biscuits. After Japan closed its doors to foreigners these techniques took on a somewhat Japanese character; but products of that time, such as Nagasaki sponge cake (*kasutera*), which is Spanish in origin, are still popular today. With the reopening of Japan to the West, some enterprising Japanese began producing Western confectionery in quantity, but with only limited success. To Japanese who were used to rice crackers and bean jam, Western candy was too rich and sweet smelling. Westerners consider milk, eggs, nuts, marshmallows, vanilla, and chocolate the proper ingredients for confectionery. Thus for most non-Japanese, it is not a mouth-watering experience to find such items as rice, beans, potatoes, leaves, and seaweed gelatin in what has been offered as "sweets."

Japanese confections are classified according to the way they are made and according to their ingredients. A major distinction is made between confectionery with a high water content (*namagashi*) and dry confectionery (*higashi*). One example of *higashi* is *senbei*, or rice crackers—although the labeling of shrimp- or seaweed-flavored rice crackers as a "sweet" comes as a surprise to Westerners. *Awaokoshi*, made with millet, is another dry confection. Some foreigners who taste it might think they are munching on birdseed, although *awaokoshi* is similar to American health-food candy bars made from sesame seeds and honey.

*Namagashi* consists of such confections as *yokan*, a sweet bean jelly that resembles the inside of a Western jellybean; *mushimono* (steamed confections) like the sweet, gummy *uiro* candy; and *manju*, buns with bean-paste filling. *Mochigashi* is another kind of *namagashi* and is so named because one of its ingredients is rice cake. In addition to all these, it is possible to find sweets like *anpan* that combine traditional Japanese with imported Western ingredients and techniques.

Foreigners are sometimes surprised to see how often Japanese give each other gifts of candy. In the West, too, of course, cookies and chocolates are given as gifts; but more often candy is bought simply to satisfy one's own sweet tooth. In this respect, Japan probably is becoming Westernized. Japanese *wagashi* meanwhile seems to be more and more a treat for older people or a gift for special occasions.

# A Selection of Japanese Sweets

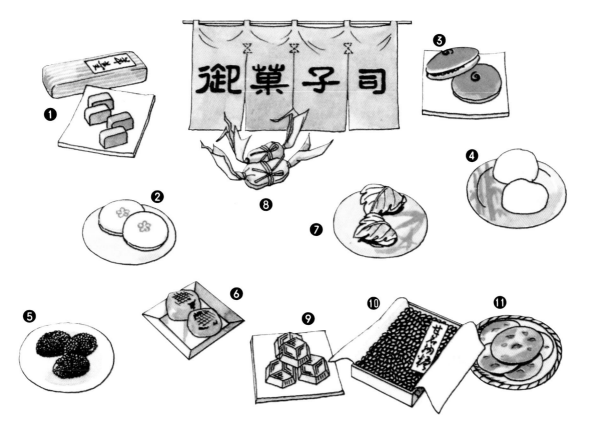

1  **yokan:** bean-paste square
2  **monaka:** bean-paste filled wafer
3  **dorayaki:** bean-paste filled pancake
4  **daifuku-mochi:** bean-paste filled ricecake
5  **ohagi:** glutinous-rice cake
6  **manju:** bean-paste filled bun

7  **kashiwa-mochi:** bean-paste ricecake with oak leaf
8  **chimaki:** sweet ricecake wrapped in iris or bamboo
9  **rakugan:** powdered beans or rice dried with syrup
10  **ama-natto:** red beans boiled in sugar water
11  **senbei:** sweetened or salted rice crackers

# KOME

## Rice

SINCE ancient times, rice (*kome*) has been the mainstay of the Japanese diet. There are two main kinds of rice in the world: the Indian type (*Sattiva india*) and the Japanese type (*Sattiva japonica*). The latter, with its short, fat grains, had become a part of Japanese agriculture by the third century B.C., the beginning of the Yayoi period.

Because rice production was the basis of Japanese society, rice culture shaped the attitudes of the people. Its importance can be gauged by the fact that rice was the main offering to the gods, that taxes were levied in rice payments, and, later, that a samurai's status was measured by the size of his annual rice allotment.

Given the central position of rice in the premodern agrarian nation, one is not surprised to learn of all the rites and rituals that were celebrated to promote and guarantee a good rice harvest. Many of these rites—indeed, most of them—persist today, although they are not as widely observed as they once were. These ceremonies may not be well known to the modern cosmopolite in Tokyo or Osaka, but they still are significant religious and social events in rural communities.

One of the most important rituals is *taue*, or rice planting, which comes at the most crucial stage of the rice-growing cycle. Initially the seeds are planted in small flooded fields called *nawashiro*. In early summer the seedlings grown in the *nawashiro* are transplanted to the more spacious rice fields. Until the invention of rice-planting machines, the work was backbreaking, requiring hours of stooping over to replant the fragile seedlings.

In the past the *taue* rites were communal affairs involving the entire local community. Tree branches were sometimes placed at the *minakuchi* (sluice gates for irrigation of the paddy), and saké was offered to the *tanokami*, or field god. After the ritual offerings had been made, the actual work of transplanting began. In some cases, the entire process was regarded as a ceremonial act. Rhythmic drumming, exuberant rice-planting songs and considerable quantities of saké helped ease the labors of the field hands.

The samurai's annual rice allotment was measured out in *koku*. A *koku* was about 180 liters and was defined as the quantity of rice that would be eaten by the average person in one year. Since the days of the samurai, however, Japanese eating habits have changed steadily. The change in the consumption of rice is especially dramatic. Before World War II each adult in Japan ate an average of 135 kilograms of rice per year. After the war, dietary habits changed drastically. Bread was introduced as a substitute for rice. At the same time the consumption of meat increased. Consumption of rice and rice based products such as saké decreased. Annual per-capita consumption of rice fell to about 110 kilograms in 1965 and had dropped to about 70 kilograms by 1990. As a result, the government has accumulated vast stockpiles of rice.

One can be misled by these statistics, however. Rice still occupies a central place in the life of the Japanese people. Although rice is no longer the chief source of calories in the Japanese diet, it is the psychological and cultural "staff of life." No meal is considered complete without it. In the Japanese home, the simple, white grains of rice served in a bowl are likely to stir up images of the home and traditional things and of the happiness and health that arise from the simplicity and dignity of everyday life.

# SASHIMI & SUSHI

## Raw Fish

"CAN YOU eat raw fish?" It is not as unsophisticated a question as it might seem. Initially many Westerners will shrink in disgust at the idea of eating raw fish. It seems to go against the injunction, drilled into them since childhood, that warns against eating in raw form anything that once was a living animal. The thought of raw meat, including that of fish, brings to mind visions from biology class of parasites and worse.

But in the Japanese mind, "raw fish" means *sashimi*—superbly fresh, artistically served, indescribably delicious. It is part of any formal, traditional dinner and represents Japanese cuisine at its best. *Sashimi* is served in slices, each small enough to be eaten in one bite. The serving is garnished with pieces of seaweed or vegetable with a small bit of *wasabi* (a hot, green root faintly resembling horseradish) on the side of the dish. With chopsticks, the *wasabi* is mixed into the soy sauce in a smaller dish, and the individual pieces of *sashimi* are then dipped into the sauce and eaten.

Many kinds of fish are eaten as *sashimi*, but the most common is tuna (*maguro*). The taste of lean, red tuna meat is incomparable, but its texture is similar to that of a very rare piece of tender beef. To the surprise of many Westerners who are trying it for the first time, *sashimi* has none of the oily "fishy" smell that most of them associate with raw fish. After all, it is difficult if not impossible in the West to purchase fish of the freshness that is considered essential in the preparation of *sashimi* in Japan.

In addition to tuna *sashimi*, sea bream (*tai*), squid (*ika*), abalone (*awabi*), and octopus (*tako*) are favorites. For those who like to combine a certain amount of risk with eating out, there is the *sashimi* that is made of the blow fish, sometimes called a globefish (*fugu*). The fish has a poison sac that must be removed with great care, and only those with expertise, experience, and a government license are permitted to prepare *fugu* for serving. A less dangerous but more

exotic *sashimi* is made from shrimp (*ebi*) that are still living—and moving about! But this kind of cuisine is only for the real gourmet.

A much more common way to eat raw fish is in sushi, probably the most typical of everyday Japanese food. The word sushi is a generic term that includes much more than raw fish. It refers to vinegared rice, shaped into mounds or rectangular blocks, with not only pieces of raw fish but cucumbers, seaweed, and pieces of egg, sweetened and cooked like an omelet. All of these ingredients and more are on display in the glass case just in front of the long wooden counter that runs the length of a sushi shop. Seated there the customer is in the best position to watch the swift handiwork of the sushi maker, who forms a mound of rice in the palm of his hand, adds a bit of *wasabi*, and then tops it with a slice of raw tuna. Or, without adding the *wasabi*, he may arrange bright orange beads of salmon roe (*ikura*) on top with a strip of seaweed around the sides of the rice. *Kappa maki*, with slices of cucumber inside, and *tekkamaki*, with a core of raw tuna, are cut from long rolls of rice that have been wrapped in seaweed.

Seated at the counter in some *sushi* shops, the customer may pay a slightly higher price for his vantage point. The set courses consist of a variety of *sushi* and have fixed prices. Served by the piece—with two pieces usually making up a serving—the prices may vary. Whatever the price, it will not be cheap. *Sushi* in recent years has become one of the most expensive foods in Japan.

# SOBA & UDON

## Noodles

INSTANT noodle products enjoy great success in Japan and in many Western countries as well. Especially for people living in big cities who may be concerned more with convenience than with nutrition, a cup of inexpensive instant noodles is ideal. But as new as the disposable packaging may be, people have been eating this kind of food for a long time. Japanese think of these cups of noodles as just one more kind of noodle dish, as the name says that it is. Westerners consider it a cup of soup. But neither noodles nor soup is a new arrival in anyone's diet.

In fact, the Japanese for many years have been eating noodles as an alternative for their staple food, rice. Originally they used buckwheat flour (*sobako*) in making dumplings which were steamed or toasted. In the Edo period the art of mixing buckwheat with wheat flour and making noodles (called *soba*) was brought to Japan by a Korean monk. Wheat flour noodles (*udon*) were first introduced from China as a confectionery with a bean-paste filling. Before noodle shops became popular, both *soba* and *udon* were sold in candy shops.

In the West, Italy is famous for its noodles. Since the Industrial Revolution made possible the production of inexpensive macaroni and spaghetti, *pasta* (the Italian word for "paste") has been the mainstay in the diet of millions of Italians. *Pasta* comes in a variety of sizes and shapes—long and short tubes, rods, ribbons and shells. The noodles are cooked typically with spicy sauces, together with ingredients like cheese, meat, fish, chicken, tomatoes, and other vegetables.

In Japan it is most common to eat noodles in soups. In the West, too, noodles are sometimes added to soups; but when they are, the noodles are in pieces that are short enough to be eaten with a spoon. To the foreigner, the Japanese custom of eating long, slippery noodles with chopsticks seems more trouble than it is worth. The foreigner who tries to learn to slurp up noodles Japanese-style finds it virtually impossible to perfect the art. The noodles are apt to whip up and hit one in the face—especially messy if the diner is wearing glasses. And the same noodles that Japanese devour with such great speed are likely to burn the foreigner's lips. Furthermore, as natural as it may be to pick up one's bowl to eat more easily, Westerners are discouraged from this habit from the time they are children. They are also taught that slurping is among the worst of manners at the table.

Japanese take great care to make food look colorful and taste good. For decoration as well as for flavor, they may place many things on top of the noodles: seaweed, mushrooms, green onion, bean sprouts, a slice of white fish sausage (*kamaboko*). Sometimes bamboo sprouts, sesame seed, and other ingredients will be added to enhance the flavor of the broth. Hot noodles are eaten all year round, of course. A hot dish that is a winter favorite is *nabeyaki udon* boiled with such things as egg, shrimp, and *kamaboko*. In the summer there is a special dish called *hiyamugi*. Served only in hot weather, *hiyamugi* is a special, thin kind of noodle that comes in a bowl of water with pieces of ice in it. But however they are eaten, whatever the season, *soba* and *udon* are traditional favorites in the everyday Japanese diet, enjoyed for lunch and for a quick snack in much the same way that hot dogs and hamburgers are standard fare for Westerners.

# MISO & SHOYU

## Soybean Paste & Soy Sauce

MISO (SOYBEAN PASTE) and *shoyu* (soy sauce) are the most important seasonings in Japanese cooking. They have been used in Japan for hundreds of years. The predecessor of *miso* originated in China about 2,500 years ago. Called *chiang* in China, *miso* was introduced to Japan by visiting Buddhist monks in the seventh century. Soy sauce has as old a tradition in China as *chiang* does, but the Japanese have used *shoyu* only during the last six centuries.

Miso is an aged, fermented soybean puree that is an all-purpose, high protein seasoning. Miso does not resemble anything that exists in the West, although its consistency is like that of soft peanut butter or firm cottage cheese. Each variety of *miso* has its own distinctive flavor and color. Miso is prized by cooks for its versatility; it can be used in soups and stews, in dips and salad dressings, or in making Japanese pickles. Misoshiru is a soup that can be eaten by itself, but it is usually a part of a traditional rice meal. The basic soup stock can contain a variety of additional seasonings and garnishes. Tofu, or soybean curd, is the ingredient most commonly used in the soup. Misoshiru holds a special place in the hearts of most Japanese. Children fondly remember their mother's *misoshiru* as something special to reminisce about. And one measure of a good wife and cook in Japan is the quality of her *misoshiru*.

The first step in the making of soybean *miso* is the soaking of whole soybeans for twelve to sixteen hours. The beans are then boiled and allowed to cool to a temperature of about thirty-six degrees Celsius. Bacteria are added to the soybeans, and the mixture is incubated for about forty-five hours. When the incubation is finished the soybeans are mixed with salt and some mature *miso*. They are then packed tightly into a vat, where the mixture is left to ferment for about eighteen months. A hole can be drilled into the side of the vat so that the *miso* can be taste-tested for saltiness to determine the proper moment to stop the fermentation process.

About 600 years ago the liquid that rose to the top of the vat during the fermentation process for *miso* was found to be a delicious seasoning. More water was added to the *miso* base mixture to obtain more of this new seasoning. The early form of *shoyu* that was obtained in this way was called *tamari*. During the Edo period *shoyu* was made from crushed soybeans and roasted barley, to which salt, water, and a fermenting agent were added. After seventy-five days of fermentation the mixture was put into coarse bags and pressed to extract the liquid. Experiments were done with other grains, but it was found that the best flavor could be achieved with a mixture of soybeans and roasted wheat .

Shoyu is the basic seasoning of sauces and dips that complement such *nabe* dishes as *sukiyaki*. When *tempura* is served, *shoyu* is part of a mixture that is added to the grated white radish that comes with the dish. Yakitori is dipped into a *shoyu*-based sauce when it is broiled, and *teriyaki* foods are basted with a *shoyu* mixture.

In Japan *shoyu* is appreciated for its subtle flavor and is used in small quantities in the preparation and eating of food. Miso can be used in the same way that salt is used in the West, although salt lacks the nutritional qualities of *miso*. The herbs and spices that are important parts of Western cuisine are often not processed but are natural leaves or plants, which have been cultivated for the seasoning they can provide.

# DEMAE

## Food Delivery Service

When Westerners want a hot meal at home but are either too tired or too busy to cook, the usual thing they do is climb into their cars and drive down to the local hamburger or fried chicken restaurant to order a dinner to take out. By the time they return home, the French fries may be soggy and the lukewarm chicken not very appetizing.

For Japanese housewives with unexpected guests or businessmen working overtime at the office, everything from a steaming hot bowl of noodles to an entire meal is only as far away as the nearest telephone. *Demae*, a delivery service offered by many inexpensive neighborhood restaurants at no extra charge, is one of the real amenities of Japanese life. Though the Japanese may take it for granted, *demae* comes as a pleasant surprise to visiting foreigners since such services have all but disappeared in their own countries.

In America, the ultimate automobile culture, low-density suburban living has combined with high labor costs to make almost any kind of home delivery service prohibitively expensive. Even the traditional home visit by the family doctor has become a rarity. And, with

the exception of the morning newspaper delivered by young boys as a part-time job and the ubiquitous pizza chains with their speedy service, home delivery of goods or services without a hefty service charge is a nearly unknown luxury.

In Japan, however, with its high population density, residential and business areas are far more concentrated and bicycles and scooters more common means of transportation. Thus the *demae mochi* (delivery persons), riding along on their bikes with heavy trays or *bento* boxes, is a common sight at lunch and dinner time in any city in Japan.

Foreigners as well as the Japanese themselves marvel at how the *demae mochi* can weave their way through crowded alleys and negotiate the sharp turns at busy intersections without spilling bowls of *udon* on trays often stacked in layers three or four high. The *demae mochi* who ride motorbikes to make deliveries often have a special rack on the back of their vehicles which swings and rocks on hinges to keep the food safe during transport.

The speedy delivery includes, along with the food, chopsticks with Japanese or Chinese dishes; and a knife, fork, and spoon wrapped in a paper napkin for Western-style food. Many housewives wash the dishes and bowls and leave them just outside the door so that the *demae mochi* can pick them up later without disturbing the family.

Like so many other aspects of traditional Japanese life, the *demae* service is changing with the times. Whereas in the past one could have the smallest order delivered at almost any time of the day or night, many shops are beginning to impose a minimum order policy and regular delivery hours. Some of the busier restaurants have even begun to charge for this formerly free service. Along with the dramatic change in Japanese eating habits since the end of the World War II, American-style fast-food chain stores which offer complete dinners "to go" are be springing up everywhere in Japan these days. One can only hope that so convenient and gracious a custom as *demae*, with its warm personal touch, can survive in the expensive, noisy future toward which modern Japan is unquestionably rushing headlong.

# PART FIVE

# Religion
# and Spirituality

心

# *ZEN*

## Zen Buddhism

ZEN HAS had a profound affect on both the religious and the secular life of the Japanese for the last seven centuries. It has also been the focus of study and concern by a great number of Westerners, especially in this century. Despite its profound influence, Zen remains an enigma to both Japanese and Westerners. The Zen experience has provided for a variety of uniquely Japanese values and life styles, but simplicity seems to be the word that best expresses the total statement of Zen. That does not mean, however, that Zen is simple to express or comprehend. Zen aims at a realization that is within the reach of everyone but that requires the personal effort of the individual.

As a sect of Buddhism, Zen came to Japan from China and reached its greatest influence during the Kamakura period, when it flourished under the shoguns. The origins of Zen stretch back to India and a monk named Bodhidharma (c. A.D. 420–534). He practiced an ascetic life and was noted for staring at a blank wall for nine years to gain enlightenment. It is the "wordless tradition" of Bodhidharma that has been passed from one Zen patriarch to another down to the present day. The word Zen means meditation and comes from the Chinese *ch'an*,

which came from the Indian word *dhyana*. For Zen, enlightenment requires an intensity of physical and mental effort that deliberately attempts to strain the individual to the point of sudden enlightenment, or *satori*.

Eisai (1141–1215) introduced both Zen and tea from China to Japan. The modified form of Chinese Zen was quickly adopted by Japan's military class, and the tea was used by the monks to maintain their alertness during meditation. However, it was Dogen (1200–53) who was the moving force behind Zen culture. His school was called Soto and his method of meditation emphasized *zazen* (literally "sitting in meditation"), which required that a particular kind of cross-legged position be maintained for hours. Under a strict code of living and with daily practice of *zazen* the disciples of Dogen sought enlightenment. As they sat in *zazen*, the Zen master might hit them with a stick to maintain their alertness. There was no guarantee that enlightenment would occur. If there was enlightenment it happened in a flash and could be verified only by the disciple.

Zen appealed widely to the *samurai* of the Kamakura period. These warriors found that the discipline of Zen complemented the strict training they needed for living in a feudal society. Zen masters followed either the Soto school, which emphasized *zazen* and the reading of the Buddhist sutras, or the Rinzai school, which emphasized concentration on the *koan*, a nonrational theme or paradox. It was not bookish knowledge that impressed the *samurai* but the qualities of discipline and concentration as expressed by the Zen masters.

The spirit of Zen is present in contemporary Japan. The Zen masters attempted to pass the necessary moral qualities to their followers, whether those disciples were monks or soldiers. Consequently those same qualities can still be witnessed today in a number of areas, from the Japanese swordsman's discipline to the flower arranger's austerity, from the tea ceremony's simplicity to the Noh actor's economy of movement on the stage. Zen has become more than a religious aspect of Japan; it reflects an approach to life itself. It is a way of life that is lived or experienced rather than one that is understood.

# Temple Grounds, a Pagoda, and Grave Markers

1  **sanmon:** the main gate of a temple

2  **hengaku:** wooden tablet with a temple's name

3  **sango:** "mountain title" of a temple

4  **shoro:** belfry with a tiled roof

5  **tsuri-gane:** temple bell hanging in a tower

6  **shumoku:** wooden clapper used to strike a bell

7  **soryo:** Buddhist priest or *bonze*

8  **koromo:** dark, loose robes worn by Buddhist priests

9  **hoshu:** "magical gemstone" used in monuments

10  **hi-bukuro:** the part of a stone lantern where a flame is lit

11  **ishi-doro:** stone lantern

12  **tsuri-doro:** small metal lantern hanging from eaves

13  **kato-mado:** a window that widens at the base

14  **hondo:** the main building of a temple

15  **gohai:** large eaves extending from the *hondo*

16  **wani-guchi:** flat, metallic gong, hanging from *gohai*

17  **mawari-en:** veranda-like porch

18  **koro-ya:** large, roorfed, stone censer

19  **sando:** stone pavement leading to a temple

20  **goju-no-to:** five-story pagoda at some temples

21  **kurin:** the nine decoratives rings atop a pagoda

22  **sorin:** term for the decorations on a pagoda

23  **gorin-to:** stupa made of stones of five different shapes

24  **sotoba:** stupa made of a long, thin wooden board

# JINJA

## Shrines

WHEN ONE thinks of the great religious buildings of the Christian West—St. Peter's in Rome, Notre Dame, Chartres—it is their architectural magnificence that first comes to mind. The soaring towers, stained-glass windows and priceless works of art create a space distinctly separate from nature and everyday life, and project images of paradise and of eternal life after death. Likewise the mosques of Islam and temples of Buddhism overwhelm the senses with dazzling tile and gold decoration, the smell of incense and the hypnotic sounds of drums, gongs and chanting priests.

The *jinja*, or Shinto shrine, is a very different kind of place because Shinto is a very different kind of religion. Usually described as a form of polytheistic animism, it has no elaborate theology, no holy books, no moral codes or precepts. Similarly *jinja* can be found anywhere because the Shinto gods (*kami*) they enshrine can be almost anything—a person, an animal, a tree, a stone. Though it is said that there are 80,000 shrines, their exact number is unknown. On the roofs of high-rise buildings, in the sea on small islands, on mountaintops or in large cities one can find *jinja*. All have the characteristic *torii*. All are places of prayer.

Most, built on raised platforms, are modest wooden structures with pitched roofs. Some have a handful of visitors throughout the year; others attract millions at New Year's or for festivals.

It is not the building itself that usually makes a *jinja*. The Grand Shrine at Ise is an extraordinary edifice with a striking architectural simplicity. The use of thatch, cedar, and other beautiful natural materials makes the Ise shrine a major touchstone of the Japanese architectural tradition. However, every 20 years for nearly 1,200 years it has been torn down and an exact replica erected. Though the design is as ancient as Japan itself, it is not the structure but the constant process of rebirth that characterizes Ise and is a main theme of Shinto.

Many smaller shrines can only be approached with some effort. One must climb a steep series of steps along a mountainside, moving farther and farther away from a local town or village. Slightly exhausted, one finally passes beneath the *torii* and comes upon a quiet grove of trees in which there is a small wooden structure. Usually one tugs on a rope to ring a bell, tosses a coin into a collection box, claps three times, and bows one's head in silent prayer. The shrine itself seems more like a road marker; it is not so much the building but the place it indicates—the grove, the stones—whose presence one feels.

At festival times the silence gives way to the noise of the crowds and chanting of young men carrying the *mikoshi* (portable shrine). On these occasions the *jinja* serves as a traditional focus of Japanese social life. Here it is the center of ancient agricultural festivals or pageants commemorating important mythological or historical events. Others center mainly around fertility rites, the worship of male and female sex organs as a source of life. Some shrines are dedicated to such phallic deities.

Ultimately *jinja* and the Shinto practices that surround them are viewed by most Japanese not as a religion at all but as a fundamental part of being Japanese. As such, what the *jinja* symbolizes is not a conscious belief to be supported by facts or disproved by arguments, but a way of life, the history of the people, their collective feelings and intuitions.

# An Overhead View of a Shrine and Its Grounds

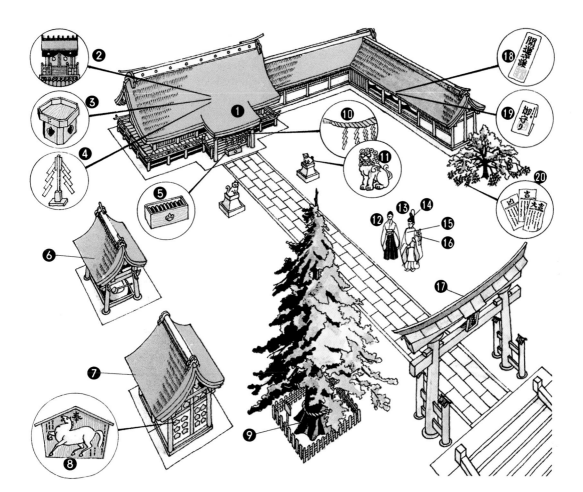

1  **haiden:** hall of worship
2  **go-shintai:** enshrined object of worship
3  **sanbo:** ceremonial wooden stand
4  **heihaku:** sacred wand with white paper
5  **saisen-bako:** offertory box
6  **te-mizuya:** water-filled basin or trough
7  **emado:** hall for a votive plaque of a horse
8  **ema:** votive plaque of a horse
9  **go-shinboku:** sacred tree
10  **shime-nawa:** sacred rope of twisted straw
11  **koma-inu:** guardian-dog statues
12  **miko:** a shrine maiden
13  **kannushi:** chief priest of a Shinto shrine
14  **kanmuri:** headgear worn by a Shinto priest
15  **ho:** formal coat worn by a Shinto priest
16  **o-nusa:** prayer-rod used by Shinto priest
17  **torii:** sacred gateway at the entrance of a shrine
18  **o-fuda:** wooden good luck charm
19  **o-mamori:** paper or cloth good luck charm
20  **o-mikuji:** prophecy written on slip of paper

# OMISOKA

## New Year's Eve

IN THE opening lines of one of his stories from *Seken munesan'yo*, translated into English as *This Scheming World*, Saikaku Ihara remarks that "It is the way of the world . . . that on New Year's Eve the night is dark." Westerners who read these lines may be puzzled, perhaps assuming that this is just a bit of gloomy philosophy about life in general. Nevertheless for Japanese before the Meiji Era, New Year's Eve was set according to the lunar calendar, so that *omisoka* was literally the "great thirtieth day," when the moon is in the earth's shadow, as the Chinese characters for the word *omisoka* suggest. Another name for *omisoka*, now sufficiently archaic that many younger Japanese may not know it, is *otsugomori*, from *tsukigomori*, the "hiding of the moon." (Since in former times the last day of the year was the traditional occasion for collecting and paying debts, it was often not only the moon that was hiding!)

New Year's Eve in Japan, like Christmas Eve in the West, tends to be preceded by feverish activity. The Japanese seem to exceed their own reputation for diligence as they rush to finish the year's work. Yet in this case, at least, the goal is clearly rest and relaxation. Many stores advertise uninterrupted business hours right up until the end of the year, but on New Year's

Eve the doors close early and stay closed for the long New Year's holiday. In Japanese homes last-minute cleaning and cooking are foremost in the minds of most family members. In earlier years baths were taken early so that the last few hours of the year could be enjoyed in utter tranquility. Many Japanese now forego this tranquility, however, to watch the "Red and White" singing contest that is aired nationwide on television during the closing hours of the year.

According to traditional belief *omisoka* is a time, like *bon*, when departed spirits return to their earthly homes. One explanation for the characters with which the traditional name for the twelfth month, *shiwasu*, is written, is that Buddhist priests were so busy going around reciting sutras for the dead that they had to run. New Year's nowadays is hardly associated with sutras in the minds of most people, perhaps because they feel too concerned with the here-and-now to worry about those in the hereafter. In fact, Saikaku somewhat humorously suggests that even in his day many people had already shifted memorial services to the summer to avoid interference with New Year's festivities. One wonders what he would have to say about those modern young people who give up family get-togethers in favor of skiing trips.

Japanese New Year's is sometimes likened to Christmas in the West. Despite differences in origin and religious meaning, there are indeed similarities in terms of the sentiments that these holidays evoke. Both holidays are traditionally family celebrations, as well as a time to remember and renew important personal relationships. Christmas tends to inspire strong feelings of nostalgia in many Westerners. For the Japanese, on the other hand, New Year's focuses attention on the future rather than the past: *Omisoka*, like *toshiwasure* (forget the year), suggests the winding up of things—settling accounts with the past and looking ahead. Nevertheless, whether one celebrates the past or the future, the holiday season marks an important milestone in one's own personal history. The Buddhist temple bells of New Year's Eve and the church bells of Christmas Eve are both reminders of a common human need for hope.

# OMAMORI

## Good Luck Charms

IN JAPAN charms, amulets and talismans are collectively known as *omamori*. Literally, the word *omamori* means to "protect" or "defend." They are intended to offer protection against a wide range of life's problems and uncertainties: sickness, shipwrecks, fires, painful childbirth, bankruptcy, and other vicissitudes.

*Omamori* are small pieces of paper or cloth on which are written the name of a god or a special invocation. *Ofuda* are a similar type of good luck charm. They are generally thin, oblong pieces of wood on which a picture of a god or the name of a shrine or temple is written. The distinction between *omamori* and *ofuda* is rather vague. Both are consecrated and distributed as good luck charms by Shinto shrines and Buddhist temples.

The distinction between *omamori* and *ofuda* seems to be based on the way in which they are used rather than on any clear-cut difference in their appearance. Originally *omamori* were kept in small bamboo tubes or worn around the neck. Nowadays they are kept in small bags (*omamori bukuro*) and worn or carried by the person desiring protection. On the other hand, *ofuda* are generally attached to the entrance gate or door of a home or placed in the family shrine (*kamidana*). Charms and amulets have their origin in ancient animistic and pantheistic beliefs which attributed supernatural powers to natural phenomena—the sun, moon, mountains, rivers, trees. To these early man directed his appeals for health, wealth, and happiness.

The use of good luck charms is widespread even in modern times. Such charms are commonly encountered among the Indians of North and South America, for example. The horseshoe displayed in some American homes is another example of this folk belief.

But compared to their Western counterparts, Japanese *omamori* are much more a part of everyday life. A holiday visitor in Japan would not think of returning home without buying an *omamori* from one of the famous temples or shrines near his vacation spot. On New Year's holidays millions of Japanese across the nation brave the crowds and long lines to pay their respects at temples and shrines and to buy their *omamori*. In an effort to help out the pilgrims and fatten its coffers, one enterprising shrine started a mail-order service for *omamori*. Sales were reported to be very good.

The outside observer may be hard put to reconcile modern Japanese city life with the ubiquitous presence of *omamori*. It is not that the Japanese people are more religious than Westerners, although they are quite tolerant of all religions. Rather, the Japanese penchant for *omamori* comes from the universal human need to seek protection and safety, or better luck in their business endeavors which is what the pilgrims seek when they exchange a small amount of money for a small, attractive object.

*Omamori* have a wide range of uses. They frequently serve as mementos of travel. They make an attractive gift for a neighbor or fellow worker. *Omamori* may be purchased for the consolation of a sick relative, to insure the good health of one's children, or the successful passing of an exam by a university hopeful. In fact, recent best-sellers have been the *omamori* designed to protect against car accidents. They may be seen dangling from the rearview mirrors of cars, taxis, and trucks. These little charms seem to do something to soothe the jangled nerves of commuting "pilgrims" as they journey home in rush-hour traffic.

# JIZO

## The Red-Bibbed Deity

WHETHER in the city or country, at busy urban intersections or quiet country crossroads, one can find statues of Jizo throughout Japan. To many Japanese he is the "stone Buddha" who acts as a silent guide through difficult times. His statue has the wishing jewel in one hand and an alarm staff in the other. His powers extend to that of guardian of the roads.

In the Christian West there was a similar guardian. A child growing up in a particularly religious Catholic family in America might have been presented a medal of Saint Christopher by his mother to wear around his neck. Although that child may have been personally ignorant of the medal's symbolic "powers," the mother's gesture symbolizes a real belief in the medal's ability to provide protection against evil.

There are a number of stories relating to the origin of Saint Christopher. Each story tells of the challenge of a believer's imagination and faith.

In like manner, the protection of Jizo has been sought by those believers who need his guardianship both in this world and the world to come after death. *Jizo*, literally translated, means "earth store" or "earth warehouse," and his image is very popular in Japan. Although he stimulated little interest in India where he originated, *Bodhisattva Jizo* (from the Sanskrit *Kshitigarbha*) gained a popular following in both China and Japan. Originally this deity is said to have been a woman in former lives. Compassion, often thought of as a "feminine" trait, is still considered one of the foremost characteristics of Jizo. Today in Japan both women and children can look to Jizo for aid and compassion. Jizo's love is ubiquitous; it encompasses pregnant women, sick children, and those who lost their lives at an early age. To each, Jizo offers spiritual assistance and personal comfort. Like the boatman Christopher, Jizo is known for his assistance to children who have died and need his help to pass safely through the nether world. Westerners may wonder at the infant's red bib or the hood that is frequently tied on Jizo statues, but it is, again, the image of a deity protecting children. Respect for Jizo spread throughout Japan from the twelfth to the seventeenth century. Jizo's popularity with the Japanese people has never faded.

Saint Christopher's popularity reached its greatest height in Europe during the Middle Ages. The Roman Catholic Church has since removed him from the scroll of the saints. What was reality to many Christians was judged by the Church to be a myth. However, myth is sometimes stronger than reality, and the legend of Saint Christopher carrying Jesus on his shoulders across a dangerous river remains fresh in many people's minds.

Likewise, Jizo has never lost his influence among the Japanese. He represents the hope and power of compassion. Mothers still pile stones neatly on Jizo's head or at his feet in the belief that the stones will aid Jizo in assisting their lost child's crossing of "the river of death" into the next life.

# MIAI KEKKON

## Arranged Marriages

PERHAPS no topic discussed today in English language classes in Japan arouses more controversy and debate than the topic of the Japanese marriage arranged through a go-between and the traditional *miai*. Many foreigners are initially repulsed by the idea and reject it totally before learning what it really means. They assume that it is cold and mechanical and is diametrically opposed to romantic love. The young Japanese who are totally opposed to the idea are equally vehement in their objections.

To some the concept of arranged marriage is closely associated with the idea sexism. Although early Japan was a matriarchal society where women held considerable power, the importation of Chinese thought and ideology changed that. During Japan's long feudal era, women took second place to their swordbearing "protectors." Their principal functions became childbearing and housekeeping. They were not necessarily equal partners of men or objects of their love. In the wealthier classes, however, parents raised their daughters carefully to be accomplished "hand maidens" of men. Depending first on family status and then upon such things as looks, poise, and knowledge of the traditional arts, young ladies became items of varying value on the marriage mart. The only true power they had was in making a "good match," and ambitious families used their daughters as pawns to bring about desirable alliances through their marriage.

It is estimated that of the one million marriages taking place annually in Japan, one third to one half are products of *miai*. Most foreigners would be horrified to hear this and would jump to the conclusion that the couple had little or no say in the matter. This, of course, is quite far from the truth. Few young Japanese today would marry anyone they did not want to marry. What arranged marriage means today is that the partners were introduced by a go-between or matchmaker. This person is usually an old friend of the family or a relative of one of the partners. The go-between decides to arrange an introduction only after carefully considering the couple's compatibility quotient. Compatibility is based upon such things as social class, wealth, educational background, and outside interests and hobbies.

In formal introductions a kind of resume or personal history, with photograph attached, is given to each individual's parents prior to the meeting of the young couple. At this stage a parent may reject a proposed match and never mention it to the child. If the parents approve, however, the personal histories are passed on to the prospective bride and groom. At this point the young people have their say. They can decline to go through with the "date," and often do, sometimes on the basis of the picture alone. Young Japanese who object to these rituals of *miai* say that they reduce human beings to a kind of merchandise, to be closely inspected for flaws. Others who are less self-conscious claim that they are a good idea, provided that each person has the courage to admit whether or not he or she would truly like to see the other person again after the meeting.

More and more Japanese, like young people all over the world, are mixing freely with the opposite sex through school, work, and friends and are finding marriage partners without any help at all from a go-between. But for those who have little opportunity to meet prospective wives or husbands the tradition serves an important function.

# *SOSHIKI*

## Funerals

IN JAPAN Shinto and Buddhism exist side by side in a kind of balance. Most Japanese follow some of the traditions of both these religions throughout their lives. Although Japan's native Shinto beliefs were firmly established long before Buddhism was imported, funerals (*soshiki*) very readily and naturally became a Buddhist function. This is partly because Shinto, with its concern for cleanliness, looked upon death as something to stay clear of. Although there are Shinto funeral ceremonies, they are seldom observed except in funerals for royalty or in other state funerals. Even Shinto priests may be given Buddhist funerals. This mixing of Buddhism and Shinto, moving back and forth between the two of them, seems quite strange to Westerners. Japanese may have a wedding ceremony in one religion and a funeral ceremony in another. For many Westerners the Christian church attends to all such spiritual needs from birth to death. This is only one of the differences between Japanese and Western customs.

For the Japanese *soshiki*, the body is dressed in a white cotton kimono and is given the appearance of someone who is going on a pilgrimage. A small purse with some coins in it is hung around the neck to aid in the crossing into the

afterlife. The corpse is laid with the head toward the north—a custom that makes most Japanese, superstitious or not, avoid sleeping with their head toward the north.

Just as some Roman Catholics have wakes for the dead, the Japanese conduct *tsuya* for those who have died. These *tsuya*, however, are observed with much more decorum and are generally much more subdued than the wakes that are associated especially with the Irish.

Funeral ceremonies in the West usually are conducted in a church or funeral home. Funeral services at home are much less common now than they are in Japan. At the Japanese funeral the foreigner might find that the Buddhist ceremony seems to give little attention to the person who has died. At the *soshiki*, friends may make speeches about the deceased; in the West it is usually part of the priest's or minister's function to make a short speech about the life and character of the person who has died. After a funeral in Japan, the body is transported to a crematorium in a jet-black hearse with a wooden roof that looks somewhat like a portable shrine—a remarkable mixture of the old and the new. Because of the Christian belief in resurrection on the last day of the world, cremation is still not very common in the West. In fact Church law traditionally has forbidden cremation for Roman Catholics. In America the dead are buried in shiny metal caskets. Americans may purchase their own caskets and cemetery plots long before they die. But the Japanese practice of buying a gravestone and inscribing one's own name on it in red strikes some foreigners as rather macabre.

In the West much of the religious tone of the funeral has been lost, and secular funerals are becoming more and more common. Once the funeral ceremony is over, it seems soon forgotten—a sentiment expressed in the finality of a phrase like "dead and buried." In Japan, however, the family gathers once a week for seven weeks following the funeral, and even many years later ceremonies are held in honor of the deceased. Westerners do, of course, remember their dead by placing flowers on graves and in churches and by offering prayers in their memory. But the Japanese commemorate death in a regular, fixed manner with more ritual.

# A Shinto Wedding and a Buddhist Funeral

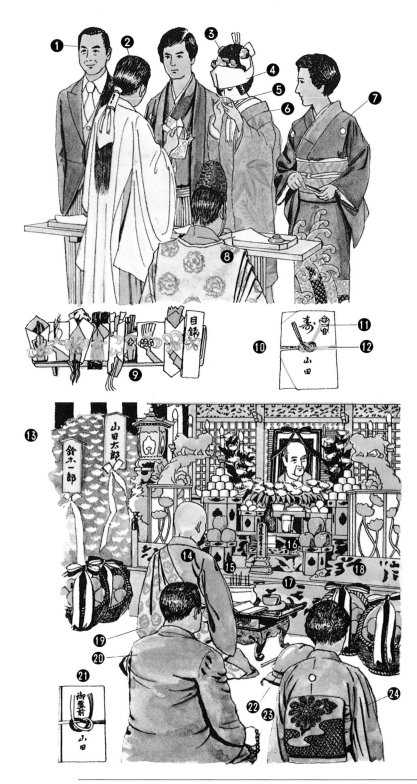

## KEKKONSHIKI

1  **nakodo:** go-between or matchmaker

2  **miko:** shrine maiden

3  **taka-shimada:** elaborate hairstyle for a bride

4  **tsuno-kakushi:** white hood to hide a bride's "horns"

5  **sansan-kudo:** ritual of taking nine sips of saké

6  **uchikake:** traditional overcoat for women

7  **tome-sode:** formal black kimono for older women

8  **shinkan:** a Shinto priest

9  **yuino-hin:** betrothal or engagement gifts

10  **o-iwai:** wedding gift, often money

11  **noshi:** dried abalone, wrapped and sent for luck

12  **mizuhiki:** stiff paper strings for decorating gifts

## SOSHIKI

13  **kujira-maku:** striped curtain for formal affairs

14  **soryo:** Buddhist priest

15  **ihai:** wooden memorial tablet

16  **kaimyo:** posthumous Buddhist name given to the deceased

17  **senko:** stick of incense

18  **saidan:** funeral altar

19  **kesa:** robe worn by Buddhist priest

20  **moshu:** chief mourner

21  **koden:** offering of money at a funeral

22  **mokugyo:** wooden gong, used in chanting sutras

23  **juzu:** Buddhist rosary

24  **mofuku:** black clothing worn in mourning

# *BUSHIDO*

## The Samurai Code

BUSHIDO, the "way of the warrior," still motivates modern Japanese thought and behavior. Some critics, in fact, consider *bushido* to be the soul of Japan.

A glance at *bushido's* roots may explain how such a sweeping statement could be made. In part, the code summarized accumulated centuries of warriors' values and rules of behavior. It glorified war, hardiness, courage and, more important, truth and loyalty to one's lord. To these practical directives were added a complex blending of philosophical thought from sources as varied as Shintoism, Buddhism, Confucianism, and the teachings of Mencius. Except for the specific references to fighting, then, *bushido* ideals were often highly idealized versions of traditional values. Perhaps it is to be expected that these extremes are recalled today as the essence of the samurai code. One

favorite literary and dramatic theme is the story of the Forty-Seven Ronin in the eighteenth century. Their feudal lord, Asano, had drawn his sword against Kira, another daimyo, within the shogun's court. For this breach of conduct, Asano was ordered to commit *seppuku*, an honorable suicide ritual. Asano's samurai became masterless *ronin*. In a carefully planned and executed plot they successfully avenged their master's death by killing Kira. The act was quite literally one of self-sacrifice since they were aware of its consequences—an order to commit *seppuku* themselves. To this day, *bushido* is associated in the minds of many Japanese with these *ronin* whose selfless devotion to their lord's honor was more important to them than life itself.

*Bushido* belongs to an era of Japanese history that ended well over a century ago. At that time, when the feudal era was brought to a close by the Meiji Restoration, many of the elite samurai class became rulers of the modern nation. They brought with them many of their *bushido* ideals—devotion and loyalty in particular—which became enshrined as examples for the entire Japanese nation. This was a factor in the widespread acceptance of militarism prior to and during World War II.

With defeat and surrender, *bushido* and the militarists were officially discredited and consigned to history. Those who attempt today to return to the *bushido* ideals of the past receive little support. Some believe that the writer Yukio Mishima had hoped to revive the warrior's ideals within the Japanese army; having failed, he chose to commit ritualistic suicide. Mishima's death attracted a great deal of attention in the West. Many Japanese, however, saw him as a rare and bizarre exception.

Even today, however, *bushido's* ideals are implicit in much of modern Japanese life, particularly in the numerous vertical relationships within business and academic life. For example, it is still common for company employees to work "for life" in companies, devoting themselves almost slavishly to a cult of work.

At home, at school, at work and even at play on the baseball field, loyalty, stoicism, devotion to hard work, and concern for the group rather than for the individual are stressed.

# PART SIX

# The Home
# and Daily Life

# NIHON KAOKU

## Japanese Houses

A LITTLE over a hundred years ago, the foreigner visiting Japan saw a kind of architecture that was unquestionably unique. If the visitor stood on a hill in the countryside the farmhouses below would have all had high, sloping roofs covered with thatch. Looking down on a city would reveal small wooden houses with walls around them, closely clustered together.

The outsides of Japanese homes were not the only things new to the foreigner's eye. Inside, the floors were made of *tatami*, straw mats covered with smoothly woven rush. Rooms could be used for various purposes. They were separated by thin sliding doors covered with paper or fabric. The side of the room bordering the outer corridor was made of *shoji*, sliding latticed doors covered with opaque white paper. Ceilings and trim were usually of light unvar-

nished wood, and its natural grain was considered to be an object of extreme beauty.

In the principal rooms in a Japanese home there was a special feature. It was the *tokonoma*, or decorative alcove. Usually it was a deep recess on one side of the room, and its floor was often made of highly polished wood. A scroll (*kakejiku*) appropriate to the season was hung on its wall, and a vase filled with fresh flowers was placed in front of the scroll. The wooden post, which reached from floor to ceiling on the side of the *tokonoma*, was chosen for its unusual shape or grain. Although resembling a structural necessity, it was purely decorative.

Regarding overall design, the principal feature of a traditional Japanese home was its modular structure. Rooms were designed to accommodate a certain number of *tatami*, usually six or eight, and the size of the mats was fairly uniform, with only slight regional differences. The standard mat size was approximately 1.8 by 0.9 meters, and the standard of spatial measure ment was the *tsubo*, the size of two *tatami* placed together with an area of about 3.3 square meters. Although *tatami* sizes vary slightly today, the *tsubo* is still a unit of measurement for houses and lots as well.

The overall effect of the traditional Japanese home was that of straight lines and uncluttered space. The sliding doors between rooms could be removed easily to form larger rooms when needed. The outer storm doors, or *amado*, could be slid back, opening the entire house to its enclosed garden. It is generally acknowledged that modern Western architecture, with its clean, rectangular design and open, airy feeling, has been influenced by traditional Japanese architectural principles.

Today, however, the Japanese-style room is fast becoming a curiosity. Homes built today often have only one *tatami* room, and many people forgo the *tokonoma* entirely because it is both expensive and nonfunctional. Although many Japanese still live on *tatami*, sleeping on *futon*, or bedrolls, and sitting on floor cushions known as *zabuton*, *tatami* is definitely on the way out. Even now, *tatami* rooms are often reserved for guests or special occasions and are otherwise neglected, especially by the younger generation.

# A Traditional Residence at Festival Time

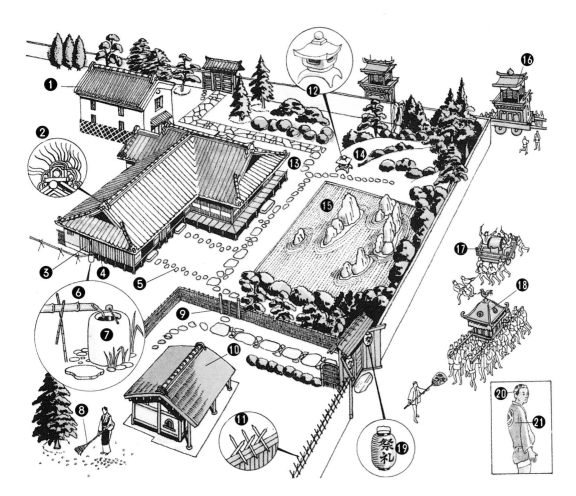

1  **dozo:** storehouse
2  **oni-gawara:** ridge-end tile
3  **to-bukuro:** storm-door closet
4  **ama-do:** outer storm-doors
5  **tobi-ishi:** garden stepping-stones
6  **kakehi:** bamboo water pipe
7  **chozu-bachi:** stone washbasin
8  **kuma-de:** bamboo rake
9  **shiorido:** garden gate made of branches
10  **hanare:** detached cottage or guesthouse
11  **shinobi-gaeshi:** fence spikes for security

12  **yukimi-doro:** stone lantern with three legs
13  **nure-en:** veranda-like porch
14  **tsuki-yama:** small, man-made hill in a garden
15  **kare-sansui:** stone garden
16  **dashi:** festival float
17  **matsuri-daiko:** festival drum
18  **mikoshi:** portable shine, or palanquin
19  **matsuri-jochin:** festival lantern
20  **hachimaki:** a headband
21  **happi:** workman's livery coat

# *ZASHIKI*

## The Japanese Room

THE GUEST room in a traditional Japanese-style house is called *zashiki*, a word that originally expressed the concept of "a room with *tatami*." Although *tatami* is commonly used as a floor covering in Japanese homes today, it did not become popular until the Edo period. Before then, rooms usually had wood floors that were covered with simple straw mats. This shows in the origin of the word, since *tatami* is derived from the verb *tatamu*, which means to "fold" or "pile," suggesting that in those earlier times the mats would be stacked to the side when not in use. For that reason the *zashiki*'s floors that were completely covered in woven rush matting made the room a very special one. *Tatami* flooring continues to be an essential and primary characteristic of the *zashiki*. Typically, the room is 6 or 8 mats in size, each mat measuring approximately 0.9 by 1.8 meters.

Another characteristic feature of the *zashiki* is the *tokonoma*, or alcove. Earlier, in the Edo period, only the aristocracy were permitted to have *tokonoma*, but from middle of the eighteenth century commoners began to adopt them in their housing. The *tokonoma* is the focal point of this sparsely but elegantly furnished room. Usually a scroll or other hanging (*kakemono*) will be placed in the *tokonoma*.

Throughout the year *kakemono* are replaced to reflect the changing seasons or to commemorate some special event. Arrangements of flowers and fine pieces of pottery or ceramics also are placed in the *tokonoma*.

One side of the *tokonoma* is graced with a support post, or *tokobashira*, made of fine wood. Typically, the *tokobashira* is handrubbed, naturally finished wood from the trunk of a tree. Other, different woods—pine, cryptomeria and cypress, for example—will be used in the construction of the *zashiki* and other rooms. But the wood of the *tokobashira* is the finest and most expensive in the entire house, often costing hundreds of dollars. Rosewood is often used, and occasionally even ebony has been used for the *tokobashira* in the homes of the very wealthy.

In the center of the room is a low table, usually of some fine wood that is lacquered or varnished. Guests sit on *zabuton*, cushions that are placed directly on the *tatami* floor. In the summer, *zabuton* with linen covers are used; in the winter, silk coverings replace linen ones. Good taste will allow very few additional items in the *zashiki*. Often the only other piece of furniture is the *chigaidana*, a set of low shelves placed at one side of the room.

Traditionally, the etiquette of the *zashiki* is as strictly controlled as its furnishings. Well-established rules of behavior exist for this room, which has been set aside for receiving and entertaining guests. By custom the guest of honor always sits in front of the *tokonoma* with his back to it. The least honored position is the one nearest the entrance of the room. Properly humble guests, no matter how important they actually may be, remain near the entrance until they are directed to the place where they are to sit.

For many Japanese the *zashiki* and its etiquette are becoming things of the past. Westernization has brought changes in the way people design and build their houses as well as changes in the way they entertain their guests. And even for those who would prefer to carry on the tradition of the past by having *zashiki* in their homes, the space and the expense required are luxuries that most Japanese cannot afford today.

# A Look into a Traditional Dwelling

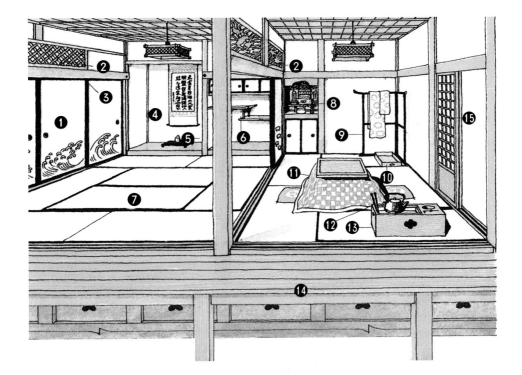

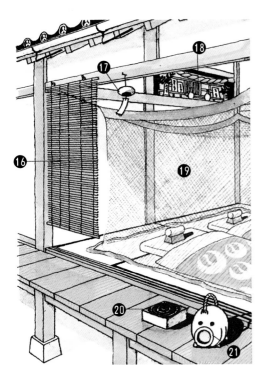

1  **fusuma:** sliding paper doors
2  **ramma:** transom
3  **kamoi:** lintel beam over a doorway
4  **tokonoma:** decorative alcove
5  **toko-bashira:** wooden post next to *tokonoma*
6  **chigaidana:** zig-zag shelves
7  **tatami:** woven rush floor mats
8  **butsudan:** Buddhist family altar
9  **iko:** lacquered wood rack
10  **midare-bako:** box or tray for kimono
11  **kotatsu:** low, heated table or foot well
12  **hibashi:** tongs for handling hot charcoal
13  **naga-hibachi:** rectangular wooden brazier
14  **engawa:** veranda-like porch
15  **shoji:** sliding paper doors
16  **sudare:** a bamboo or reed curtain or blind
17  **furin:** a hanging wind chime or bell
18  **kami-dana:** shelf for a family's Shinto shrine
19  **kaya:** mosquito netting
20  **katori-senko:** coil insense, a mosquito repellent
21  **ka-yari:** earthenware pot used for *katori-senko*

# A Look into a Standard Japanese Kitchen

1  **take-zaru:** bamboo basket
2  **saibashi:** long chopsticks for cooking
3  **kama:** iron pot for cooking rice
4  **tsukemono-ishi:** stone weight for pickling vegetables
5  **donburi:** large bowl used for dishes like *katsudon*
6  **wan:** lacquered wooden bowl
7  **dobin:** ceramic teapot
8  **jubako:** stacked lacquerware boxes
9  **choshi (tokkuri):** thin-necked saké container
10 **sakazuki (choko):** small saké cup
11 **hakama:** coaster-like stand for *tokkuri*
12 **hashi:** pair of chopsticks
13 **chawan:** rice bowl used for everyday meals

14 **kyusu:** teapot, smaller than a *dobin*
15 **chataku:** saucer for a teacup, usually wooden
16 **zen:** lacquered tray
17 **o-hitsu:** wooden container for cooked rice
18 **handai:** wooden tub for making sushi rice
19 **shamoji:** rice scoop
20 **seiro:** wooden steamer
21 **masu:** square box for meauring saké and grain
22 **waribashi:** plain disposable chopsticks
23 **ko-bachi:** small bowl
24 **suriko-gi:** wooden pestle
25 **suri-bachi:** cone-shaped earthenware mortar
26 **makisu:** bamboo mat used for rolling foods
27 **hashi-oki:** chopstick rests

# NIHON TEIEN

## Japanese Gardens

PERHAPS the one feature of Japanese culture that has been most widely exported and copied abroad is what people all over the world have come to call "Japanese" or "Oriental" gardens. Indeed, there are few parks in the major cities of Europe and America that do not have at least one corner set aside for some variety of a Japanese garden. Despite this widespread popularity, not many people can fully describe just what a Japanese garden is. It seems to be one of those things in life that are hard to define, but which almost everybody can recognize at first glance.

Actually the experts classify Japanese gardens, or *nihon teien*, into three distinct categories. The oldest and most common type is the landscape garden. According to Japanese chronicles, this art was first introduced to the country in 612, when a Korean gardener was invited to Japan to landscape a park at the southern end of the imperial palace in Kyoto. Varying in size from tiny "postage stamp" plots tucked in among the houses and buildings of crowded cities to large and enchanting parks that attract thousands of visitors each year, landscape gardens attempt to imitate what the the five elements of nature: the mountain, the river, the sea, the forest, and the field.

Through a skillful blending of artificial hills; rocks and boulders; pebble lined "rivers"; real or imaginary "ponds"; and a wide variety of trees, shrubs, and plants, the landscape garden attempts to create both the visual and spiritual impression of the totality of nature. Such gardens belie the careful planning and meticulous attention to the precise layout of their design; instead, they manage to suggest a random, untamed and an almost haphazard quality that attempts to mirror nature itself. Unlike the well-ordered and symmetrical look of many European-style formal gardens, Japanese landscape gardens reflect a belief that nature is not subject to predictable or well regulated patterns.

The second category of Japanese gardens is the stone or rock garden. This uniquely Japanese contribution to the art of landscaping can lead to raised eyebrows or puzzled expressions among Western tourists, and even many Japanese will admit that its appreciation is an acquired taste. Developed during the Muromachi period under the strong influence of Zen Buddhism, rock gardens consist of little more than a few large rocks standing in what appears to be forlorn isolation on a bed of carefully raked pebbles. Usually enclosed in walled courtyards with little or no greenery to soften the effect, rock gardens symbolize to the viewer the endless and unchanging nature of the sea. The simple, austere character of the garden is meant to foster contemplation and meditation.

The third category of Japanese garden bears a closer resemblance to conventional landscaping forms in the West. Known as tea-house gardens, these are usually small, enclosed gardens adjacent to tea houses or special rooms in which the Japanese tea ceremony is performed. They are designed to provide the quiet, peaceful atmosphere necessary to enhance the ritual. Although tea-house gardens do not necessarily include the five elements of nature featured in landscape gardens, they still emphasize a natural harmony among trees, shrubs, rocks, and water—most often in the form of a small well or spring. In all the categories and varieties of Japanese gardens, however, the essence of appreciation is not only visual but spiritual and psychological. They reflect a theme of Japanese thinking in which form is as important as function and where mood and spirit add to an appreciation of beauty.

# SENTO & FURO

## Baths

IT IS EVENING. The streetlights have just flickered on. In the glow of a streetlight ahead a Japanese woman and two small children can be seen. They are not strolling but are walking with quick steps and seem to be moving toward a definite destination. A closer look reveals that they are carrying what appear to be small plastic basins under their arms. They turn and enter a large wooden building with a well-lighted entry, remove their shoes and put them into a small locker, then disappear behind a door. There are other people in the entry, all of them carrying the same kind of small plastic basin. The women go behind the door on the right and the men behind the door on the left. Those leaving, alone or in a family group, are dressed casually in *yukata*, and many have wet hair. This is the *sento*, or Japanese public bath.

A *sento* can be found in nearly every neighborhood in Japan. Although most new houses

and apartments have a *furo*, or home bath, the *sento* is still an essential element of daily life for many in Japan. Taking a bath is only one of the reasons Japanese go to the *sento*. In a unique way, the *sento* is a place for socializing and relaxing.

*Sento* in Japan today are segregated—women on one side, men on the other. Small children enter either section, depending on which parent they accompanied. Soap, towel, and other bathing essentials are carried in the plastic basin. Inside the segregated portions of the building, there is a room for disrobing. After the bather removes all his or her clothes and places them in a basket in the dressing room, the next step is to enter the large, tiled bathing room. One sits facing the wall, on a small stool situated by faucets for hot and cold water, and washes quickly. After this perfunctory washing, it is usual to enter the tub for a short soak. The bather soon leaves the tub to do a more thorough scrubbing, then reenters the tub for a much longer soak. The tub—sometimes the size of a small pool—is usually very hot. Some Westerners find the temperature quite uncomfortable. Once in the tub, the bather's movements are limited, not by lack of space but by the heat of the water. The hot water of the *sento* can relieve much of the day's anxiety: troubles seem to be carried away in the steam rising from the water.

The skin tingles and is often quite red when the bather finally leaves the tub. Normally, one quickly dries off, and after retrieving the clothes left in the basket and dressing, it is a simple matter to retrieve one's shoes and head back for home, prepared in mind and body for a good night's sleep. Japanese sing its praises but the Westerner may be unprepared for several aspects of the *sento*. The social atmosphere, the lack of privacy, the custom of scrubbing outside the tub and then soaking for a long time are quite a contrast to Western bathing.

The *furo* in the Japanese home resembles the *sento* in many ways. It is smaller, of course, suitable for only one or two adults at a time. The tub is filled once with hot water and the family members each scrub and soak in turn. As in the *sento*, all washing is done outside the tub, which is only for soaking and relaxing.

# HARI & KYU

## Acupuncture & Moxibustion

WHAT DO needles, moxa, and fingers have in common? The answer is simple: They are all forms of Oriental therapy used to relieve aches, pains, tension, fatigue, and symptoms of disease. In acupuncture, or needle therapy, sharp, very thin instruments of gold, silver or platinum are painlessly inserted into the flesh. In *kyu,* or moxibustion, small cones of wormwood are ignited against the skin. In *shiatsu,* finger pressure is applied to the body. Until the nineteenth century, these ancient Chinese practices were widely used in Japan. Today, however, Western medical science predominates. As a result, *hari, kyu,* and *shiatsu* therapists function somewhat on the periphery of the medical profession as quasi-medical practitioners.

Ironically it is the Western medical world that is now beginning to take an interest in Oriental healing arts. In many countries researchers are examining the promising aspects of acupuncture therapy, particularly now that more information on the subject has come out of China. One of the reasons for previous resistance to Oriental medicine was the almost insurmountable gap between Eastern and Western medical theory. Some Chinese medicine is based on ancient cosmological beliefs. Modern Western medicine, on the other hand, has traditionally relied on empirical evidence.

If one particular part of the body malfunctions, a Western doctor treats the affected part. An Oriental therapist would prefer to treat the whole body. The Chinese believe that the same energy that underlies the matter and movement of the universe is contained in its microcosm—the body. As this energy is divided into two opposite but complementary forces, the *yin* and the *yang,* a balance between the two is necessary for sound health. *Hari, kyu,* and related techniques help reestablish this balance.

Western doctors have always acknowledged the sometimes miraculous results achieved by Oriental therapies. But they have had difficulty accepting the explanations that lie behind the practical treatments. Even if these physicians believe that the points used to insert needles or burn moxa were mapped after careful observation, they are uncomfortable with the fact that no measurable and systematic explanation based on dissection or chemical analyses can be found. Acupuncturists work from complicated charts on which are marked "meridian lines." The bases for these imaginary lines are about 600 *tsubo,* or acupuncture points. Because the body's energy is said to flow along the meridians, manipulating the special points should unblock these channels, allowing the affected areas to be properly supplied.

Thousands of sufferers, particularly those with chronic complaints such as headaches, rheumatism, or neuralgia, know that *hari* and *kyu* have worked where drugs and surgery have not. But their voices are not strong enough to convince licensed physicians that these therapies should be used in place of accepted Western approaches to pain and disease. Thus many patients are denied a form of sedation without the unpleasant side effects of drugs, they miss the kind of relaxation that accompanies the control of hyperactivity, and they are unable to alter many unpleasant conditions due to malfunctioning physiological systems. Meanwhile, research into these centuries-old therapies continues. If that research can successfully analyze the reasons that *hari* and *kyu* work, more physicians will accept Oriental medicine as a part of universal medical knowledge.

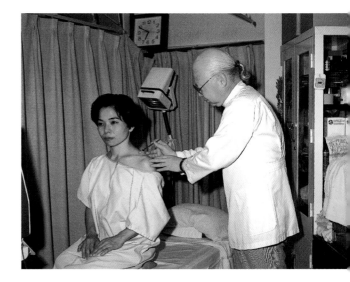

# SEIBO & CHUGEN

## Summer & Winter Gift Giving

THERE are many occasions for gift-giving throughout the year both in Japan and in Western countries. The most important of such occasions in Japan are *seibo* (between December 13 and 28) and *chugen* (before the peak of summer, usually during July). In the West, exchanging gifts is a custom commonly associated with Christmas. Since they fall at about the same time of the year, Christmas and Japanese *seibo* offer several interesting points of comparison.

Christmas, though a Christian holiday, is related historically to the celebration of the winter solstice and the beginning of the New Year. The custom of exchanging gifts is commonly associated with Saint Matthew's account of the Wise Men bringing gifts to the baby Jesus. Yet here too the custom is probably older than Christianity. As in Japan, offering a present was to some extent a token of congratulation for having survived yet another year as well as an expression of hope for continued prosperity.

A more specifically religious parallel can be drawn between Christmas and *chugen*. Originated in China, *chugen* stands "between" *jogen*, January 15 in the lunar calendar, and *kagen*, October 15 in the lunar calendar, though these dates are of lesser significance in Japan. The custom of gift-giving seems to have partially grown out of the practice of making offerings

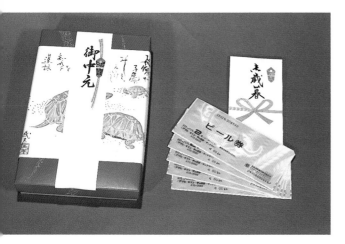

to one's ancestors. Likewise, Christians often explain Christmas gifts as a symbol of gratitude to God for the birth of Christ.

Nowadays there are frequent complaints that all three traditions, Christmas, *seibo*, and *chugen*, have lost much of their meaning under the weight of modern affluence, materialism, and commercialism. Christmas for millions of Americans represents many hours of hectic shopping in crowded shopping centers. Many Japanese, too, feel trapped by obligations to those with whom they have business and formal social ties. Gift-giving under such circumstances is hardly a spontaneous gesture but rather a carefully calculated measure of one's social and economic position. Anxiety about miscalculation or misunderstanding may be just as much a troublesome factor as the money one has to spend. The mountains of boxes and fancy wrapping paper that accumulate around the garbage cans toward the end of December and July are cited by social critics as a symbol of extravagance and ostentation.

Bemoaning society's preoccupation with mindless pleasures and material possessions is itself a sort of holiday custom. The Puritans of the seventeenth century succeeded in banning Christmas merrymaking in England and the North American colonies as pagan wickedness. In Japan the excesses of New Year's celebrations have been ridiculed by a number of writers, including *haiku* poets Basho and Buson as well as the Meiji-era novelist Natsume Soseki. Every year many Americans resolve to make Christmas a quiet, family time, with greater emphasis on the religious and spiritual meaning of the event. Likewise, many Japanese make an effort not to be caught up in the more irksome aspects of *seibo* and *chugen*.

Part of this impulse may relate to memories, whether accurate or not, of a more innocent childhood. After all, much of both the joy and frustration of holidays lies in nostalgia. In Japan the contrast can be clearly seen in the difference between *otoshidama*, relatively small amounts of money given to children at New Year's, and more expensive *seibo* lavished upon company executives. And even the most jaded adult in Europe or America can be inspired by the wonder in a child's eyes at Christmas.

# KISSATEN

## Coffee Shops

ASSUMING that tea is the nonalcoholic drink of preference in Japan, foreign visitors are sometimes surprised to discover that coffee shops are almost as common in Japan as bars. Their surprise often turns to shock when they are asked to pay $4.50 for a cup of this Japanese brew.

The keen observer will soon realize, however, that for $4.50 at a Japanese coffee shop one buys space, time, and a certain atmosphere as well as a cup of coffee. In large cities where living space is at a premium, and meeting or entertaining friends at home is unusual, the *kissaten* provides space to do just that. For the price of a cup, hours may be spent talking, reading, or even studying without fear of waitresses asking one to order something more or leave.

The modern Japanese *kissaten* still exhibits some of the features of the Meiji-era café from which it—as well as bars—developed. Coffee drinking, like so many Western habits that entered Japan over a hundred years ago, was felt to be both modern (i.e., advanced and progressive) and somewhat exotic (i.e., foreign). At the Meiji café, surrounded by Western decor, one could sample such then-exotic drinks as milk, European-style tea, and coffee, the preparation of which was be the job of an expert.

At a first-class coffee shop each cup is prepared individually from freshly ground beans. The cup, along with the creamer and sugar bowl, is placed before the drinker with a sense of precision and decorum reminiscent of the studied gestures of the tea ceremony. Moreover, a large number of specialized books on coffee brewing containing information on preparation, temperature control and the blending of beans can be found at many bookstores.

This tendency toward specialization extends to the place in which the coffee is served. In France, a country with its own unique coffee house tradition, the café is an intensely social, even political institution. In Paris a typical coffee shop extends out into the street; the famous sidewalk café blends both public and private spaces. Cafés are often characterized by their patrons whether they be students, political activists, or those from the arts. People frequent a certain café to see others as well as to be seen.

In Japan, however, the sidewalk café is almost unknown and many coffee shops are located in windowless basements of buildings. One reason for the difference is a lack of space. But also, Japanese seem to view the coffee shop as a sort of personal refuge for withdrawing from the world for a period and relax in privacy.

Another result of the emphasis on personal preference is the extraordinary diversity of coffee shops. While most Parisian cafés look more or less alike, many Japanese coffee shops have atmospheres that seem almost custom-made for a certain kind of patron.

The *kissaten* that specialize in music provide a good example. There are jazz, folk, rock, *chanson,* and classical coffee shops, each of which features only one kind of music, sometimes live but usually recorded.

*Manga kissa* provide the lovers of comic books with an enormous collection including rare back numbers which they can peruse at their leisure. The list can be extended, but in the *wafu* (Japanese-style) *kissa*, coffee enters a traditional environment and has come full circle from the fashionable Meiji café. A century later, a heavy, oily brown liquid, made from beans grown almost 20,000 kilometers away in South America, has taken its place in the timeless world of bamboo, *kimono*, and *koto* music.

# FUROSHIKI

## Wrapping Cloths

HAVING postponed Christmas shopping until the last minute, and looking for something beautiful, characteristically Japanese, and light enough to be sent cheaply all the way to the U.S. by airmail, a foreign resident in Japan hit upon *furoshiki*. He bought five or six and sent them off to friends in California and New York, wondering what their impressions of these beautifully decorated, all-purpose wrappers would be. On a recent trip back to the States, he reported that one friend in New York was using the one-square-meter *furoshiki* as a table cloth, while another in California had mounted a smaller *furoshiki* on a frame and was displaying it as one would a painting.

Though surprising at first, on second thought it seemed quite reasonable that non-Japanese might find original uses for these beautiful but extremely practical pieces of cloth. There are pictures dating back a thousand years showing woman carrying articles wrapped in cloth on their heads, and ceremonial clothing and relics were stored in cloth wrappings but the tremendous popularity of *furoshiki* in their present form probably dates from the institution of public baths. These came about as a fire-prevention measure in the 1600s when private baths were essentially banned. Hence *furoshiki* (literally "bath spread") is said to have been developed during the Muromachi period as a

cloth for spreading on the floor while dressing and undressing at the public baths and as a wrapper used to hold the clothing guests removed while bathing. The endless number of designs made it possible for their owners to identify the cloths easily. Since then *furoshiki* have come to be used to wrap lunch boxes, decorate gift boxes, carry bottles of saké, and even to wrap *futon* when moving to a new house. There are a variety of classes offered to foreign residents to introduce the art of tying the *furoshiki*, so that afterwards the cloths can be used for practical purposes.

The variety of fabrics, from the simplest cotton to expensive silk, and the enormous range of designs make *furoshiki* a common feature of Japanese life, found in the humblest home as well as at the most elegant formal ceremony. There are classical patterns to match certain functions, and it seems that nearly any kind of *kimono* silk would be appropriate. One can even order *furoshiki* made with one's family crest, or with special words or phrases printed on it to commemorate an important event. In the older commercial areas of traditional "downtown" Tokyo (*shitamachi*), shops selling *furoshiki* are easily found and are popular with tourists seeking a unique gift and with local residents and travelers. Today it is common to see men and women carrying parcels of all sizes on the train wrapped and tied with elegant style.

Though the paper bag and plastic shopping bag seem to be replacing the *furoshiki*, especially in the cities, the advantages of the *furoshiki* should be obvious. In fact, it is hard to see why this idea never ocurred to the Western world, seeing as how the *furoshiki* is so useful. It can be used to carry odd-shaped objects easily, and when no longer needed it can be folded neatly and put into a pocket. Besides its obvious beauty it can be used over and over, while paper bags are easily damaged and soon discarded. Wet a *furoshiki* and it won't tear; when it gets dirty it can be laundered, pressed, and reused. In these conservation-minded times when so many of the habits of the "throwaway" society are being rejected, we may have something of value to learn from the Japanese customs surrounding the use of this simple piece of cloth.

# GETA & ZORI

## Footwear

LEGEND has it that when the Europeans first met the Japanese they were surprised to discover people with only two large toes on each foot. True or not, this story readily attests to the fact that the Japanese have always had a way with footwear. Though foot binding, an old Chinese custom, never became popular in Japan, the Japanese have invented an intriguing range of footgear from the rustic *waraji* and formal *zori*. Perhaps the earliest form of *geta* were the snowshoe-like footwear called *tageta*, which were made for working in paddies and common in use from the Yayoi period (ca. 300 B.C.–ca. A.D. 300). The ultimate form of these classical wooden sandals found expression in the 30-centimeter-high platform *yujo geta* worn by courtesans in the Genroku period (1688–1704). The latter were so high that the wearer, a frail young woman already weighted down by a heavy silk *kimono* and an elaborate wig, needed two assistants just to help her walk.

Even the more common variety of *geta* and *zori* seem to impose a certain discipline on the wearer. Not having grown up with them, the foreigner finds that the wearing of *geta* and *zori* have few advantages and many disadvantages. Though they do keep one's feet out of the mud on rainy days, *geta*—just like high-heeled shoes—are definitely not for climbing stairs. They can be worn with informal Western- or Japanese-style clothes but any serious walking is likely to produce blisters where the thongs rub against the bare toes. Perhaps one of the main attractions of *geta* is not their comfort to the wearer but the sound they make. Like the wooden clappers that introduce a Kabuki play or the rattle of the last train at night, it forms one element in the score of sounds that are an intimate part of life in Japan.

*Zori* and sometimes *geta* are worn with *tabi*, the kind of two-toed stockings the early visitors from the West supposedly mistook for two-toed feet. Unlike *geta*, *zori* are formal and are worn only with kimono. The kind of *zori* worn by women are normally made of leather or silk brocade, and feature a wedged heel. The *zori* worn by men are generally thinner, with a flat heel and are covered in the same kind of rush matting that is used to make *tatami*. Kimono require that women constantly walk with the toes pointing inward to avoid showing their bare legs. It is still considered ladylike, and charmingly feminine. In the West, however, this would be described as "pigeon-toed" and considered a physical disability. In Japan, when performed on stage by an actress or by geisha, walking—and even more, running in this style (*uchimata*)—seems like a strange mixture of dancing and acrobatics, a graceful but somewhat dangerous balancing act.

*Geta* can be worn with blue jeans and since both *geta* and *zori* will continue to be worn as long as Japanese wear kimono and *yukata*, they seem to be holding their own against the flood of Western-style casual shoes. Track shoes, a recent import from America, have won over a sizable proportion of the youth market. However, most Western-style shoes cannot be put on and taken off as easily as their traditional Japanese predecessors. During an average day, most Japanese get in and out of their shoes far more often than Westerners do. So one often sees the sturdy backs of shoes crushed after a few months of being leaped into and out of in the *genkan*. These days one also sees many new kinds of domestically produced "shoes" in the most astonishing shapes, made of wood, leather, plastic and even wire mesh, which attests to the continuing creativity and independence of what the Japanese put on their feet.

# KIMONO

## Kimono

ALTHOUGH Japan's status as a modern, industrialized country is well known, the word "Japan" still conjures up exotic images in the minds of many. When they hear it, they picture lovely women clad in elegant kimono, standing against backdrops of landscaped gardens, ancient temples, and narrow, lantern-lit lanes. Many first-time visitors are often slightly disappointed to find that much of Japan, especially its cities, looks very Western and that its citizens dress much the same as people do the world over, but with a different sophistication and sense of style.

The tourist wishing to see large numbers of people wearing traditional Japanese garb had better be in Japan during New Year's, go to a Japanese wedding, or attend some other formal affair. Otherwise, most of the *kimono* on display may be seen in Ginza shop windows or on view at the National Museum in Ueno.

Of course traditional Japanese clothing, being loose-fitting and comfortable, has hardly disappeared from the fashion scene. Men and women who wear Western dress during the day often change into casual kimono when at home or visiting friends. Older women tend to wear

kimono of the subdued tones and patterns considered suitable for people of their age. On summer evenings, however, light cotton kimono called *yukata* are worn by young and old alike. Most Japanese women have at least one good kimono in their wardrobes and these, however rarely worn, are well taken care of.

Many foreign women are initially astounded by how expensive a good formal kimono can be. They learn that those made of heavily embroidered, intricately dyed or specially woven fabrics can run into thousands of dollars, becoming an investment only a handful of foreigners would even consider making for a single article of clothing. What they fail to realize, of course, is that to a Japanese, formal kimono are much more than mere apparel, to be discarded the next time the fashions change. Often they are looked upon as precious heirlooms and are handed down from generation to generation. This is possible because the kimono has retained the same basic design for hundreds of years. Unlike Western clothing, it is not made to fit the individual wearer. The material is cut in straight lines with no attention paid to the curves of the body, and fitting is done each time the garment is put on.

The kimono shares a common aspect of design with the traditional Japanese house in that it too is made up of standardized parts or modules. These are four: the sleeves, body, neckband, and front panel, or *okumi*. Because of this, kimono making—as opposed to the weaving, embroidering and dyeing of kimono fabrics—is much easier to master than the art of Western tailoring. The rules governing the making of kimono have to do with such subtleties as the angle of the neckband and the length of the sleeves, details that are indistinguishable to the untrained eye. Likewise, the way a kimono is worn is of the utmost importance, and often a second person or "dresser" is required to help tie cords, adjust the sleeves and neck and wind the wide *obi*, or belt.

The second definition given for kimono in many English dictionaries is "a loose dressing gown" and tourist shops sell these adapted robes only to visitors; they are never worn by Japanese. But few foreigners would have the patience to put on and wear the real thing.

# Women's Kimono in Various Styles

1  **fukura-suzume:** special way of tying an *obi*
2  **furi-sode:** young woman's long-sleeved kimono
3  **nuki-emon:** pulled-back collar
4  **otaiko:** drum-shaped *obi* knot
5  **homon-gi:** semi-formal kimono
6  **han-eri:** replaceable neckband or collar
7  **obi-age:** band of silk to keep *obi* tied in place
8  **obi-dome:** sash clip made of ivory, wood, etc.
9  **obi:** sash for a kimono
10 **ohashori:** tuck at the waist to adjust a kimono

11 **tabi:** Japanese socks, with split toes
12 **kohaze:** metal clasps or hooks on *tabi*
13 **hakkake:** kimono lining
14 **hanao:** toe thongs on footwear
15 **zori:** sandal-like footwear worn with *tabi*
16 **hakoseko:** decorative brocade wallet
17 **obi-jime:** cord used to hold *obi* in place
18 **pokkuri:** young woman's lacquered clogs
19 **e-baori:** short overgarment for women
20 **michi-yuki:** traveling coat worn over kimono

# Kimono Accessories, *Yukata,* and Children's Kimono

1 **kara-kasa:** oil-paper umbrella
2 **ashida:** high, wooden clogs for rainy days
3 **tsuma-kawa:** toe covering for *ashida*
4 **kappo-gi:** apron with sleeves
5 **nenneko:** short coat for a pregnant woman
6 **kintaro:** baby's pinafore
7 **yukata:** informal cotton kimono
8 **kata-age:** tuck at shoulder to adjust children's sleeve
9 **sanjaku:** unsewn *obi* of soft cloth
10 **okumi:** outer front panel of a kimono

11 **uchiwa:** round, non-folding fan
12 **tsuma:** bottom corner of a kimono
13 **hada-juban:** cotton kimono underwear
14 **koshi-himo:** waist-cord for adjusting a kimono
15 **date-maki:** narrow sash worn over underclothes
16 **suso-yoke:** underskirt worn with *hada-juban*
17 **naga-juban:** long undergarment for kimono
18 **mushi-boshi:** airing of kimono
19 **tato-gami:** thick paper for wrapping kimono
20 **tammono:** woven kimono cloth

# Men's Kimono and Traditional Clothing

1  **ki-nagashi:** men's casual kimono style
2  **awase:** lined kimono
3  **kaku-obi:** stiff sash or waistband for men
4  **furoshiki:** square wrapping-cloth
5  **setta:** type of *zori* with leather soles
6  **hitoe:** unlined kimono for warm weather
7  **kasuri:** kimono with patterns woven in
8  **heko-obi:** simple *obi* worn by men
9  **geta:** wooden clogs
10  **mon-tsuki:** formal kimono with a family crest
11  **mon:** family crest
12  **haori:** outer coat worn over kimono

13  **himo:** pair of braided cords for tying *haori*
14  **hakusen:** ceremonial white folding fan
15  **hakama:** skirt-trousers, like culottes
16  **shokunin-sugata:** artisan's apparal
17  **hara-maki:** woolen waistband for men
18  **momohiki:** tight-fitting trousers for laborers
19  **jika-tabi:** split-toed shoes, shaped like *tabi*
20  **hanten:** short garment worn over kimono
21  **tanzen:** padded kimono for cold weather
22  **jimbe:** thin, summer half-kimono
23  **chan-chan-ko:** sleeveless, padded short-coat

# *YOBIKO*

## Cram Schools for Examinations

WESTERN romantics often claim that in spring the heads of young people are filled only with love. In reality, between April and June, there are term papers to be handed in and final examinations to pass. In Japan, the situation in the spring is similar, at least for one particular group. These are students from upper secondary school who wish to continue on to university. Spring for them is synonymous with *shiken jigoku*, or "examination hell." Those who successfully enroll in prestige universities are almost guaranteed preferential treatment by prospective employers after graduation. Difficulties in Japan's modern economy have only increased the pressure on students to outperform their peers in the race for the dwindling number of good jobs available. But for many of the unsuccessful the future is less rosy.

Many problems surround university entrance selection in Japan. First and foremost, too many students concentrate on certain universities—in particular the more prestigious national ones such as Tokyo or private ones such as Keio and Waseda. As a result, competition is fierce, with many students failing to advance directly to university after upper secondary school. Dubbed *ronin* (masterless samurai), this group can decide to leave the system

entirely, to enter universities that were their second or third choices, or to simply try again. Those who choose to try again spend one or more years at special cram schools called *yobiko*, where individualized programs are drawn up to try and match strengths and weaknesses with particular university entrance standards.

The odds against succeeding on an entrance examination are high. Many parents encourage attendance at a different kind of cram school called *juku* in an effort to increase their child's chances for acceptance in the university of their choice. The more ambitious mothers have even been given a special name: *kyoiku mama*, meaning "education mothers."

But whatever the inherent drawbacks of the system, Japan's present school program has met the needs its Meiji founders created it for. Japan wanted a literate, well-educated work force in order to become a leading industrial state. It achieved its goals and in the process it also made education a tool for determining status and function within society. Education, therefore, took the place of birth and class as social determinants. Inevitably, though, as the number of students in the system has increased, so has the pressure on students to graduate from schools that promise the best career chances. More students compete for severely limited places. Consequently more *ronin* attend *yobiko*, more students succumb to examination pressure and fall ill or take their own lives, and some regular teachers even exploit examination hell by accepting teaching jobs at cram schools.

Education officials are aware of both the strengths and weaknesses of the system, and changes are being introduced gradually. Like American universities the Japanese national universities, at least, are now accepting the results of standardized achievement tests as an aid to screening candidates for their own entrance exams. This decision may well produce a ripple effect on lower grade-level curricula. Standardized tests that measure the necessary abilities and aptitudes for university work ultimately shift curriculum emphasis away from the rote memorization of facts toward more creative, independent thought. This shift could in turn lead to a de-emphasizing of entrance exams.

# TAIRYO YUSO

## Mass Transit

MANY PEOPLE are aware of the fact that Japan has the most highly developed mass-transit system in the world. The most famous aspect of this system is, of course, the *shinkansen* or "bullet train" which can travel at speeds of 270 kilometers per hour or more. But there are many other things about Japan's transportation system that most foreigners are not aware of.

Consider Tokyo's subways. Although a New Yorker can rightfully boast of having the world's most extensive subway system, the same person would notice its many shortcomings after riding Tokyo's underground network of trains. First there is the noise factor. In New York, the earsplitting screech emitted by the average Manhattan train often causes people to put their fingers in their ears for protection. On several Tokyo subway platforms, on the other hand, one can hardly hear the train pull in.

Next, there is a difference in cleanliness. New York subway cars and stations are dirty. Often they are covered with colorful writing called "graffiti," spray-painted by vandals despite attempts by the police to stop them. Seats in subway cars are often defaced, and newspapers and other litter usually cover the floors. By comparison, Tokyo subway stations and cars are impeccably clean.

Perhaps the best thing about the subways in Tokyo is their regular service. In many other major cities in the world, one can stand on a platform for twenty and sometimes thirty minutes waiting for a train. In Tokyo, one seldom has to wait more than five minutes. Service, however, is not round-the-clock, and most trains stop running shortly after midnight. New York subways, which run all night, may be more convenient, but they are also much more dangerous. At least one policeman is needed to patrol each late-night train, but robberies and other crimes still occur on deserted platforms and in stations. Tokyo subways, in contrast, have few crime problems. Like all other public transportation facilities in Japan, they are renowned for their safety and their punctuality.

On the negative side of things, however, there is the rush hour. Besides adopting the English term, the Japanese have given it a new meaning. In Tokyo, it could be called the crush hour. In New York while commuting to and from work by subway, one often has enough elbow room to turn the pages of a newspaper. On a Tokyo subway at peak hours, however, this is impossible. Even though trains run every two minutes, they still carry more than twice as many passengers as they were designed to accommodate. Few foreigners are able to forget the first time they were "helped" onto a train in Japan by a professional platform pusher.

Although eastern urban centers in the U.S. have highly developed public transit systems, most other parts of the country rely almost exclusively on the automobile. In Los Angeles, for example, buses are the only available means of public transportation. Their service, however, is slow, and routes are not extensive. One can wait more than a half an hour for a bus.

In many parts of America, it is possible to eat, see a movie, make a bank deposit, attend a religious service, and even attend a funeral without ever getting out of the car. On the average, Americans spend 90 percent of their transportation money on their cars and consider them a necessity rather than a luxury. When such people visit Japan, they are quite surprised to learn that it is faster and more practical to use mass transit than risk getting stuck in one of Tokyo's famous traffic jams.

# JISHIN

## Earthquakes

OF ALL the natural disasters that afflict people the world over, none is quite as awesome in destructiveness as an earthquake. In fact, until the twentieth century the greatest of human disasters—war—was scarcely a rival, as the Japanese know all too well. In Kamo no Chomei's *Hojoki*, for example, no mention is made of the war between the Taira and the Minamoto, though we do find a vivid description of the terrible earthquake of 1185. Kamo no Chomei's catalog of such disasters is gloomy enough, but of earthquakes he writes: "Of all there is to fear, that which is most fearful is earthquakes." Though the Tokugawa period was free of the destruction of war, earthquakes and fire killed tens of thousands of people. More recently, in the Great Kanto Earthquake of 1923, more than 130,000 people were killed and missing, and in Kobe the 1995 Great Hanshin Earthquake leveled much of that beautiful port city.

Earthquakes have had a powerful effect on our imagination not only because of their incredible destructiveness but also because of their unpredictability and our previous lack of knowledge regarding their cause. It is therefore not surprising that such calamities have often been explained as a form of divine punishment. Nichiren, for example, blamed the

natural disasters of his time on the degeneration of Buddha's Law (*mappo*). In the West we find a similar idea in the apocalyptic visions that conclude the New Testament: The seventh and final disaster by which the world is to be judged comes as a massive earthquake.

For the Japanese, earthquakes represent not only a potential threat of utter destruction but also a fairly routine reality. For foreigners who are relatively unaccustomed to feeling the floor suddenly shake or seeing the ceiling lamps begin to sway back and forth, the occurrence of an earthquake can be a rather frightening experience. Their Japanese friends may take the event much more calmly and may become excited only if the quake is quite severe. Perhaps ironically, they may feel especially safe on the upper floors of tall buildings, since these are carefully designed to withstand the earth tremors. A Japanese businessman was recently heard to marvel at a massive building in the northeastern United States with connecting wings unsupported by pillars from the ground. He remarked that in Japan such a building would be impossible, for nowhere in Japan is there a region secure enough from the danger of earthquakes.

In the United States, San Francisco is probably the city that is most like Japan in terms of an "earthquake mentality." As in Japan, there are strict building codes, but lurking in everyone's mind is the knowledge that a massive earthquake could cost thousands of lives. Scientific estimates combine with occasional occult warnings of coming destruction. Yet in Japan, at least, fatalism is yielding to an increased sense of optimism about the ability of scientists to predict earthquakes and hence to minimize the numbers of people killed. Of course total accuracy may lie far down the road, but in the meantime there is increasing public awareness of the need to prepare for such disasters. The Japanese government has sponsored programs to inform the people of what they should do during and after an earthquake. Recent increases in the purchase of earthquake survival supplies and equipment are an indication of a growing determination to face the possibility of disaster with cool heads and common sense by being prepared.

# PART SEVEN

# Communication and the Printed Word

# KANA & KANJI

## The Written Language

OFTEN, the first contact that tourists have with written Japanese is when they look at the menu in their hotel's coffee shop. The first thing they notice is that it looks very different from, say, a menu in San Francisco's Chinatown. If the tourist studies the menu closely it will be obvious that many Western items on the menu, like coffee, are written in a simple syllabic script. If such visitors have a flair for solving puzzles and breaking codes, they may even be able to teach themselve the rudiments of *katakana* before finishing their meal. Proud of this accomplishment, they will be quite disappointed when a Japanese points out that *katakana* is a phonetic syllabary used mainly for foreign words adapted to the Japanese sound system.

If the tourist picks up a Japanese newspaper to look at, another discovery will be made. There are three entirely different kinds of writing, all mixed together. One will quickly notice that in addition to Chinese characters or *kanji* there are numerous cursive symbols that are similar to *katakana* in simplicity. A Japanese friend can explain that this is *kana*, too, but a different kind from what was seen on the menu. It is called *hiragana*, another complete syllabary of the Japanese language. *Hiragana*, it will be explained, is used to write Japanese word endings, such as verb suffixes denoting

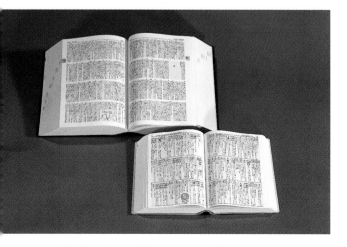

tense. If the visitor stays in Japan for a while it will become apparent that *hiragana* is used in dictionaries, children's books, and comic books. By this time the visitor may have given up any hope of ever learning to read Japanese.

The complexity—and thus the difficulty—of Japan's writing system is rooted in history. Before Chinese characters were imported to Japan around the first century, the Japanese had no written language. Then, at first, they wrote in Chinese while continuing to speak only Japanese. Because of obvious difficulties, they eventually tried to use Chinese characters phonetically, ignoring their meaning, to write Japanese. This phonetic use of characters was called *man'yogana*. Japanese soon developed a dual system of reading *kanji*. The *on* reading was an approximation of the Chinese pronunciation; the *kun* reading was a direct translation of the character into Japanese. Thus the character for person, for example, was given an *on* reading of *jin* or *nin* and a *kun* reading of *hito*, the Japanese word for "person."

In Chinese each character represented one monosyllabic word. Since most Japanese words are polysyllabic, two or more characters were usually needed to write one Japanese word phonetically. Because this was so time consuming, two simplified styles were developed for writing characters. *Katakana*, developed by monks, is more angular. *Hiragana*, a cursive phonetic syllabary, was used in the late tenth and early eleventh centuries by ladies of the court to write love letters, poems, and diaries.

Although the number of Chinese characters in daily use was restricted to fewer than 2,000 after World War II, the Japanese writing system is still a formidable one. One way of simplifying it would, of course, be to abandon Chinese characters in favor of *kana*. But a great number of Japanese words are pronounced exactly the same way. With such homophones it is sometimes necessary to see the words written in characters in order to understand their meaning. Writing English in phonetic symbols, so that the words "there," "they're," and "their" would be written the same, would present similar problems. In Japanese, where homophones abound, the confusion and misunderstandings would be far worse.

# NAMAE

## Japanese Names

A FOREIGNER relates his experience of being introduced to a lot of people named Suzuki and Nakamura when he first came to Japan. To tell them apart, he spent a great deal of effort trying to learn their first, or "given," names. This proved to be both surprisingly difficult and an unnecessary waste of time. Japanese themselves almost never use first names, preferring on all but the most intimate occasions to use the surname and a title, or even the title alone. First names in Japan are not exactly secrets, but there is a strong reticence about using them.

This near-secrecy is only partially broken by the custom of exchanging name cards (*meishi*). Although name cards contain the full name of the bearer, their primary purpose is to proclaim the bearer's status. It would be considered bad form to read the given name from the card and then use it to address the person it names. Such an attempt might also be very embarrassing because the characters used in Japanese names have notoriously variable pronunciations. The single character for one common first name, for example, can be read in seven ways: Hajime, Hitoshi, Hajimu, Makoto, Masashi, Osamu, or Susumu. As a component in a first name it has no fewer than sixteen possible readings. Some two-character given names have more than one hundred theoretically possible readings. It is not surprising that even well-educated native speakers of Japanese can quite often do little more than guess about the correct pronunciation of a first name.

Western surnames very often are derived from the occupations of distant ancestors, like Smith, Cooper, or Thatcher. In Japan, however, there is almost no connection between occupation and surname. Until 1868 only warriors and nobles, whose "occupation" could be equated with their status, were allowed to have surnames. This changed suddenly when the Tokugawa regime fell. Surnames were no longer forbidden to commoners and they usually chose surnames that were related to nature, to agriculture, and to geographical features near their homes. The characters for village, field, river, forest, cliff, beach, island, valley, bridge, and other terms that refer to local landscape appear constantly in Japanese surnames. With a little practice foreigners can teach themselves to recognize Japanese surnames most of the time.

The naming of a child in Japan is an extremely complicated process. Few new parents in Japan fully understand what is involved, so most consult outside experts. In America the primary consideration in selecting a name is its sound. There is something unpleasant about a name like Hulda Snerd. Meaning is also occasionally a problem; the name Fanny Tubbs is but a mild example. In Japan there are more factors to be considered. First of all there is the law. Not all *kanji* may be used in names. Fewer than 2,000 *joyo kanji* (characters in daily use), plus a few dozen other *kanji*, prescribed by the government, can be used in names. The sound of the name is important, of course. And the meaning is much more important than it is in America or Europe, because the potential for puns and off-color meanings is far greater in the Japanese language than in any Western language. The large number of homonyms in Japanese makes Japan a punster's paradise.

If parents do a particularly bad job in name choosing, the child may eventually change that name to a more propitious one. Fortune-tellers in Japan routinely analyze and judge the balance of their customer's name in a process called *seimei handan*. If the name is judged unlucky, a change will be suggested.

# *HANKO*

## Personal Seals

THE BEGINNING of the Japanese movie "Woman in the Dunes" is unique. As the credits roll by on the screen a seal appears beside each name. Each seal is a different size and shape but they are all *hanko*, name seals, showing that each artist involved in the movie has personally signed his work.

The *hanko* is an important part of everyone's life in Japan. It serves the same purpose as a written signature does in the West, and it is legally binding. Most Japanese own at least two *hanko* and sometimes as many as six or more. The two most common are the registered seals (*jitsuin*) used for important contracts, loans, and other official business; and the personal seals (*mitomein*) for home use. The *jitsuin* are specially designed, and no one is permitted to register more than one of these seals. The jitsuin is normally placed directly below one's signature and in many cases a certificate of authenticity will have to be presented at the time of use. *Mitomein* can range from ready-made cheap ones to handmade expensive ones.

The *hanko*, or *inkan* (seal impression), comes from China. Legend has it that an emperor of China presented a Japanese king with a golden seal (*kinin*) 2,000 years ago. A golden *inkan* dating back to the fifth century has been found in Kyushu, confirming the use and importance of these seals in ancient times. *Hanko* made of gold are not in use today. Some people still feel, however, that the material from which the *hanko* is made, as well as the way it is made, can affect their destiny. There are shops and mail-order houses that will recommend the best material and size for a person's *hanko* after taking into consideration the date of birth and the number of strokes in the *kanji* used for the user's name. Some of the most auspicious materials are, the horn of water buffalo and the wood of the box tree, but crystal, bamboo, and stone are also used. A strong material is usually chosen to prevent the edge from breaking—a bad omen that presages a loss of money. The Chinese characters in a name are carefully studied and arranged to fit the eight sectors of the *hanko*'s circular surface: success, happiness, fate, health, confidence, management, love, and money. A 15-millimeter registered seal is recommended for men, a 13.5-millimeter seal for women. For both men and women, an 11-millimeter personal seal is generally considered the best.

A different kind of seal is used in the West, employing thick sealing wax and a metal signet that usually has an initial or some other design on it. These seals were often made in the form of rings and were worn by kings and other potentates. Now they are bought and sold as antiques and accessories. Japanese *hanko* and *shuniku*, the thick red ink that they require, sometimes fascinate foreign visitors. Many tourists buy antique *hanko* as souvenirs, and sometimes they have their names translated into *kanji* to be put on *hanko*. A considerable amount of care must be taken in the choice of characters used to represent foreigners' names, however. In the case of the name "Barton," an unknowing tourist chose the characters *ba*, meaning "horse," and *ton*, meaning "pig." Fortunately the *hanko* maker was kind enough to suggest a gentler *ba* that meant "leaves" and a *ton* that meant "sincerity."

# MEISHI

## Business Cards

THE BUSINESS card, as it is known today, originated in the West. It is used more in Japan, however, than in any other country in the world. The foreigner visiting Japan sees people exchanging *meishi* in coffee shops, hotel lobbies, and even on the street. The newcomer often jumps to the conclusion that every Japanese citizen has cards. Of course this is not true.

Young people, nonworking housewives, and blue-collar workers seldom need to have *meishi*. Most people who are associated with a company, organization, club, or professional group, do have them. These make up a large percentage of the group-loving Japanese population.

More surprising to the foreigner is the fact that people carry their cards everywhere, the way Americans carry credit cards. At first, this seems awkward to the non-Japanese. A flat billfold does not have a special section for cards, and the Westerner cannot figure out where to keep them. If foreigners want to have good business relationships in Japan, however, it is imperative that they quickly learn the rules of the game. They learn that forgetting to put business cards in their pockets can be more troublesome than forgetting his wallet.

Carrying one's own cards is not the only new habit the foreigner in Japan must acquire. One must also learn how to file efficiently all the *meishi* that are soon collected. Many newcomers voice the opinion that the standard address book is a more practical way to record names and telephone numbers. They soon realize, however, that the *meishi* file has many advantages. Cards can be added, removed and refiled easily. With the traditional address book, information must be erased or crossed out and corrected as people change jobs and phone numbers. Eventually a new book is needed. Rewriting everything is a job most people dread as much as filling out their income tax returns.

Perhaps the most important role that *meishi* play in Japan is in the initial business meeting.

Everyone exchanges cards, so everyone can relax. No one has to worry about forgetting a name or a title, because it is all written down in black and white. Some foreigners, however, do not find this custom relaxing at all.

The Japanese businessman will receive a card and carefully read it. If he sits down, he will place the card in front of him. During his conversation he will look at the card now and then, checking the information it contains.

At this point the foreigner begins to feel uncomfortable. There may be a feeling of being evaluated or even ignored. It can be hard to understand why a little card is competing with its owner for attention. The foreigner does not yet know that the *meishi* is being treated with great courtesy and respect.

In most countries a person who presents a card does not expect one in return. After having a talk with a new business contact, it is often appropriate to offer a business card. This is not a signal for the other person to offer a card in exchange. It is not uncommon or impolite, however, to ask for a card directly with, "May I have your card?"

Those in the West who have a real need for business cards have them, of course. Salesmen leave their cards after calling on customers, and secretaries are often asked to pass on cards to their busy bosses as an introduction. This is usually followed by a telephone call.

Freelancers, such as commercial artists and writers, frequently have originally designed, eye-catching cards that advertise their personalities and creativity.

# SHIMBUN

## Newspapers

IF YOU ask the average American which daily newspaper has the largest circulation in the world, the chances are the answer will be *USA Today*, the *Wall Street Journal*, or the *New York Times*, the three newspapers in the U.S. with the highest circulation. Yet, amazingly, they are outsold by not one but five Japanese dailies.

The circulation level of Japanese newspapers is indeed staggering. Whereas the full-sized *USA Today* and the tabloid *Times* have daily circulation figures between 800,000 to just over a million, the *Yomiuri Shimbun* sells almost ten million, the *Asahi Shimbun* over eight million and the *Mainichi* more than four million copies a day. These three, with the *Sankei Shimbun* and the *Nihon Keizai Shimbun,* account for a total circulation of nearly twenty-six million.

Perhaps the primary reason for the massive sales of Japan's top dailies lies in the country's land size and population density. Both the U.S.

and Japan have high literacy rates, and the newspaper industries in both nations face approximately the same amount of competition from television. Whereas Japan's readership is concentrated into 372,300 square kilometers, America's newspaper buyers are scattered over 25 times that area. Nationwide distribution is impractical, and as a result, America's leading dailies, with the exception of the *Wall Street Journal* and *USA Today* are all regional.

Although a leading American daily contains two and sometimes three times as many pages as its Japanese counterpart, in terms of content there are few real differences between the two. One of the most notable points of divergence is the tendency of American papers to feature stories about domestic affairs—and local ones when possible—on page one, while Japanese papers almost always print a considerable amount of foreign news in that space. Another difference is that while an American paper will tend to run a full page of comics every day, the Japanese will often carry a serialization of a popular novel.

Newspaper publishers in both countries consider themselves "guardians of liberty" and sometimes take vigorous and independent stances. Whereas the Japanese press remains neutral at election time, however, most American dailies openly endorse a particular candidate in their editorial columns. Some of these consistently lean toward one of the two major parties, Republican or Democratic. Occasionally their editorial opinion is reflected in stories that purport to be regular news coverage. One unusual feature of the Japanese newspaper world is the existence of the sports daily—in reality a combination of sports, entertainment, recreational, and cultural news. The over-five-million circulation of Japan's sports dailies would particularly surprise the Western reader, since in the U.S., for example, there is not even one comparable daily available—nationwide or regional. In most cases, Western sports fans who want their statistics as in-depth and as up to-date as those published in the *Hochi Shimbun* or *Sports Nippon* is out of luck. They have little choice but to wait for the weekly Sunday edition of their favorite papers with their expanded sports sections.

# PART EIGHT

# Places and Sights

# FUJI

## Mount Fuji

MOUNT Fuji's name is taken from the aboriginal Ainu word for fire, *fuchi,* and for good reason: Fuji has erupted eighteen times in recorded history, the last time in 1707. After that eruption, Tokyo (then called Edo) was covered with 15 centimeters of ash. Although almost two centuries have passed peacefully, the people in the town of Fujiyoshida at the foot of the mountain offer prayers to the Fire God at the end of August each year to keep the peace.

Mount Fuji remains the symbol of Japan throughout the world, in all its varieties: bare in summer, hidden in mist, or covered with snow.

Perhaps a gentler image to perceive, especially before climbing Fuji, is that of a sacred mountain, inhabited by the Goddess of Flowering Trees, or Spring. Her energy will help you scale the 3,776 meters. There are six popular routes—the Yoshida, Kawaguchiko, Shoji, Gotemba, Subashiri, and Fujinomiya trails— all of which are divided into ten sections of varying lengths and each with a station. The length of these trails ranges from 15 to 25 kilometers. The ascent takes five to nine hours, the descent three to five hours. Most climbers ride to the fifth station to begin their trek late

in the afternoon. They climb at night and reach the summit in time to witness the sunrise.

Mount Fuji is officially open only during July and August, and more than 300,000 people a year take advantage of the climbing season. At times it seems that all 300,000 are with you on the trail. The slopes begin to resemble the Tokyo rush hour—vertically. There is a saying that a wise man climbs Fuji once, but only a fool climbs it twice. When you are actually halfway up the mountain you begin to feel less and less wise.

At the fifth station, where most climbers begin, the atmosphere is jovial. Everyone is making last-minute preparations, buying work gloves, flashlights, and other supplies at scalpers' prices. The most important purchase, of course, is the walking stick, which will be branded in black at each station along the way to the summit, where the coveted red brand will be added at the top of the stick. The stick comes with two bells and a choice of flags.

After one last bowl of *udon* for luck, you're off to conquer the mountain. If you start at night you quickly become aware of a stillness in the air, more like a powerful aura, punctuated by the sounds of boots scrambling over the rocks. With only a flashlight beam to guide you, and with the pressure of the crowd around you to keep you moving, your jovial mood changes to a more serious concern for survival. The stations seem hours apart, and you begin to feel you can no longer go on. It seems futile—so much more to climb, so many people, it's getting so cold. The shelter looks very inviting. Why not? You pull off your boots and climb into one of the wall-to-wall barrack-style bunk beds. The wind is howling outside, but suddenly the crowd is awake and everyone is straining to look out through the tiny windows. It's almost sunrise! The purple clouds give way to a huge copper ball, rising higher over the horizon. You're going to make it. Just two stations away.

In the bright sunlight the scene is disappointing—so barren, so littered with tin cans and bottles, it hardly seems worth it. And then suddenly you reach the summit. A spectacular view stretches out in all directions and you conquer the mountain of dreams.

# KYOTO

## The Old Capital

WHEN VISITORS finally reach Kyoto they feel that they have truly arrived in Japan. Tokyo is a surprisingly huge and sprawling, modern city that is superficially indistinguishable from dozens of other cities. The exotic flavor of Japan promised by the tourist brochures is well hidden in the big-city bustle. But in Kyoto, at last, reality approaches the visitors' mental picture of Japan.

Probably the visitor is only vaguely aware of the city's distinguished past. If one does a bit of research, however, it will be discovered that Kyoto became the capital of Japan in 794, when the Emperor Kammu moved from Nara to Kyoto. The new capital was called Heian-kyo, or Peace Capital. Although not always the actual seat of government, it remained the imperial residence until 1869, when the capital and the court moved to Tokyo.

It is natural to respond to the ancient buildings, lantern-lit streets, and the occasional sight of a *maiko*, or apprentice geisha. When walking along in the streets or staying in a *ryokan* the visitor feels the peculiar sensation of entering another age and another world. Even the hills that surround Kyoto reinforce this impression inspiring the feeling that, unlike Tokyo, Kyoto is contained within natural boundaries and that Kyoto is a city that could be known and understood if one had enough time.

The visitor begins to explore the temples, shrines, and gardens with great enthusiasm. The Golden Pavilion, Ryoan-ji, the Moss Garden, and the Heian Shrine probably head any tourist's list; each delights, and gently suggests moving on to another. However, the cumulative effect of temple viewing is overwhelming: Many fall victim to a malady known as "temple-itis." The ailment is characterized by aching feet, the conviction that the last three places looked exactly alike, and the strong desire to do anything but look at another temple.

Fortunately Kyoto is a diverse city, and there are wonderful alternatives to sightseeing. Antique hunting, for example, attracts serious collectors and window-shoppers alike. The shops of Kyoto are filled with the luxuries and wares of bygone ages. Throngs of people crowd the paths around the shrine, buying *tansu*, tools, folk crafts, ancient dishes, second-hand household goods, old silk kimono, and almost everything else. No doubt some of the prices are high, but whatever the price, purchases made there are somehow twice as satisfying as similar purchases in a modern store. The carnival atmosphere, the outdoor setting, the bit of haggling over the price, all contribute to the visitor's enjoyment of the experience. If the dust is a bit thick, the dish chipped, or the old silk frayed, it only adds a new dimension to the imagined past of the item. Anything seems like a good bargain.

Upon reflection, there will be a recognition of what Kyoto shares with Paris, Rome, Leningrad, San Francisco, and a few other magical cities: the quality of mystique. Because they exude an elegance, an air of sophistication and cosmopolitanism, these cities exert a strong influence on both citizens and visitors. They are cities with supreme self-confidence, each sure that it is the best in the country, if not the world. Each enhances the visitor's perceptions of its assets while blurring visions of its faults. Thus the traffic jams and clutter around Kyoto Station are soon forgotten while the charms of Pontocho and the peace of the Zen gardens are readily recalled.

# TOKYO

## The Eastern Capital

URBAN planning is as old as the city itself. About 8,000 years ago, the citizens of Jericho built around their city a wall that still stands over twelve feet high. In Europe it was the Romans who first built totally planned towns. Those towns usually were built on a square plan. A central crossroad led to the four gates of the city wall, on the north, south, east and west sides. Behind their protection, trades and crafts reached a high stage of development.

During the Middle Ages, small towns began to appear all over Europe, around the castles of nobility. The layouts of these towns varied. They were square, circular, and even triangular. All, however, were surrounded by walls, many of which are still standing today.

In contrast, most Japanese cities and towns had no surrounding walls. The defense system of the castle was made up of moats, dirt embankments, and walls of people—samurai. Blocks of different classes of warriors encircled the castle at all times, with the most powerful living in the inner ring and the poorest on the outer edge. Temples were built in strategically important places so that their buildings could

be occupied by soldiers in case of attack. Even the streets of castle towns were designed defensively. They were short and straight, turning at right angles and creating a labyrinth that would confuse an invading force.

Because of Tokyo's present unplanned appearance, it is difficult to believe that at one time it was totally planned. It was designed as a castle town nearly 400 years ago by the powerful *daimyo* (later shogun) Ieyasu Tokugawa. In 1590, when Ieyasu first came to the Kanto Plain to establish his headquarters, there was nothing but a grass-covered rural area. Edo was nothing more than a tiny fishing village with about 100 small cottages. The castle was small and in need of repair. It had neither stone foundations nor stone walls and its roof even leaked.

Ieyasu quickly rebuilt the castle and designed his town around it in blocks. People who worked at the same jobs lived in the same blocks. Many parts of the city took their names from the occupations of those who lived there. Quite a few of these names are still used, perhaps the most famous being Ginza.

With the Meiji Restoration the imperial family moved from Kyoto to Edo and renamed the city Tokyo, meaning Eastern Capital. The new government encouraged the modernization of the city. The undeveloped area around Tokyo Station gradually became a business center with wide avenues and red brick office buildings. In most residential areas, however, the feeling of the old city remained.

In 1923 the great Kanto earthquake destroyed much of old Edo forever. New Tokyo was much more modern, with office buildings constructed of steel-reinforced concrete. During World War II extensive firebombing again destroyed a large part of the city. Although it was an excellent opportunity to plan and build a city that suited modern needs, that was not done. Buildings were crowded together haphazardly. Sewage systems were not modernized, and little thought was given to the city's future needs for gas, water, and electricity.

Because of Tokyo's unusual history, the face of old Edo has changed completely. Only around the palace can one sense the order and simplicity of design of Ieyasu's castle town. There the real Edo remains untouched by time.

# MINATO MACHI

## Port Cities

BECAUSE Japan is composed entirely of islands her relationship with the sea has been an intimate one. Today Japan's merchant fleet is one of the largest in the world, and her ports are models of automation and technological efficiency. Three port cities are also of interest to tourists and are visited by thousands every year. They are unusual in Japan because of their rich and colorful histories and are still considered to have exotic and international atmospheres.

The city of Nagasaki, located on the northwest coast of Kyushu, is known for its beautiful natural harbor. What makes the city different is that it is Japan's oldest open port. Portuguese traders first arrived in Nagasaki in the mid-sixteenth century, and soon the city became the center of Christianity in Japan. Spanish and Dutch traders also visited the port, and Japanese traders made it their homeport for trade with China, the Philippines, Thailand and other Asian countries.

Because of a general ban on Christianity, the Portuguese and Spaniards were expelled from Nagasaki in 1639. Only Dutch and Chinese traders were allowed to remain, and the Dutch were confined to Dejima, a small man made island in the harbor. During Japan's seclusion of more than 200 years, foreign learning filtered into the country only through this port. Today the city is a favorite of tourists because of its lovely scenery, historic sites, and general romantic appeal. Chinese temples, a Gothic-style cathedral, winding cobblestone streets, and European-style buildings give it an atmosphere that is unique in Japan.

The port of Kobe was opened to foreign trade in 1868. Until then the town had been little more than a fishing village neighboring the old port of Hyogo. Located on the north shore of Osaka Bay, Kobe is now one of the largest ports in Japan. Although it is connected to Osaka by three other cities that help make up the Osaka-Kobe Metropolitan Area, Kobe's atmosphere is quite distinctive. Unlike Osaka, a wholesale center and city of merchants, Kobe has an exotic appeal that attracts hordes of visitors. It has a number of "international" restaurants; and its main shopping streets, some of them roofed, sell items from the four corners of the globe. The Great Hanshin Earthquake in 1995 damaged much of the city, but rebuilding efforts have been successful in restoring Kobe's position among Japan's key port cities.

Yokohama, too, has an exotic international appeal. In 1853 Commodore Perry dropped anchor off Uraga, south of Yokohama. A year later he returned to deliver a letter from the president of the United States to the ruler of Japan. Under the provisions of the treaties they concluded, Yokohama was opened to foreign trade and foreign residents in 1859. A portion of the city was even leased to foreigners. Like the other port cities, Yokohama also has its historic foreign cemetery, a popular tourist attraction. The shops that today line the fashionable shopping street of Motomachi attract many Tokyoites and others who shop for the latest Western fashions. The city's Chinatown contains over 70 Chinese restaurants and about 20 small shops selling Chinese foods and spices.

Today the chief interest in the port cities of Kobe, Yokohama, and especially Nagasaki is historic. The significance of these cities as trade centers has been reduced in recent years as large industries—most notably steel manufacturers and oil refiners—have constructed their own pier facilities, but an island nation like Japan will always have a need for ports and harbors.

# LIST OF WRITERS

**James H. Buschhoff**
Haiku
Go & Shogi
Nihon Ryori
Miso & Shoyu

**Harold R. Dailey**
Tango-no-Sekku
Zashiki

**Charles M. DeWolf**
Setsubun
Onsen
Omisoka
Seibo & Chugen
Jishin

**Suzanne P. Firth**
Hanami
Aki Matsuri
Nihonga
Bushido
Hari & Kyu
Yobiko

**C. Goosmann**
Washi
Kendo & Kyudo
Geisha
Origami
Hanko
Fuji

**Joseph LaPenta**
Ikebana

Také
Pachinko
Demae
Jinja
Kissaten
Furoshiki
Geta & Zori

**Laura A. Martin**
Yakimono

**Richard F. May**
Kome
Omamori

**Joel Scheiman**
Hina Matsuri
Bon
Shodo
Sumo
Janken
Wagashi
Soba & Udon
Soshiki

**W. Stevens**
Sashimi & Sushi

**James Svatko**
Chanoyu
Zen
Jizo

**Raren Svatko**
Sento & Furo

**Alice Volpe**
Kabuki
Judo & Karate
Ryokan
Miai Kekkon
Nihon Kaoku
Kimono
Tairyo Yuso
Kana & Kanji
Meishi
Shimbun
Tokyo
Minato Machi

**Linda Unckless Waters**
Kyoto

**Neil L. Waters**
Namae

**Wm. B. White**
Shogatsu
Shichi-Go-San
Noh & Kyogen
Bunraku
Hogaku
Hanafuda
Nihon Teien